..... only if w

MIDDLESE
RAMBLE

lots of love

Alan

Other counties in this series include:

Other Walking Guides available from Countryside Books:

MIDDLESEX RAMBLES

Fourteen Country Walks around Middlesex

Leigh Hatts

———————

With Historical Notes

COUNTRYSIDE BOOKS
NEWBURY, BERKSHIRE

COUNTRYSIDE BOOKS
3 Catherine Road
Newbury, Berkshire

ISBN 1 85306 074 7

Sketch maps by the author
Cover photograph from Mill Hill taken by John Bethell

Produced through MRM Associates Ltd., Reading
Typeset by Clifford-Cooper Ltd., Aldershot
Printed in England by J. W. Arrowsmith Ltd., Bristol

FOLLOW THE COUNTRY CODE

Enjoy the countryside and respect its life and work
Guard against all risk of fire
Fasten all gates
Keep your dogs under close control
Keep to public paths across farmland
Use gates and stiles to cross fences, hedges and walls
Leave livestock, crops and machinery alone
Take your litter home
Help to keep all water clean
Protect wildlife, plants and trees
Take special care on country roads
Make no unnecessary noise

Contents

Introduction

Middlesex is fortunate to possess so many open spaces, so close and convenient to London. It was that closeness to the city which attracted great figures of the past to build their mansions and parks out in the then countryside - many of which are now open for us to enjoy. This book describes a wide variety of walks, reflecting Middlesex's great diversity - the stately Thames, the Grand Union Canal, magnificent Hampton Court, rural Harefield, ancient Enfield Chase, and many more.

When Middlesex County Council was abolished in 1965 most of the area was placed under the new Greater London Council. But the name lives on as a postal address for those placed in the county of London but outside the numbered postal districts and it remains a geographical name in the north and west London boroughs of Enfield, Harrow, Hillingdon, Ealing and Hounslow and Surrey's Spelthorne - the latter being one of the six Middlesex Hundreds recorded in the Domesday Book. Potters Bar, thanks to Enfield Chase, is part of Old Middlesex whilst Chipping Barnet to the south has always been considered to be a Hertfordshire town. Under modern local government boundaries however, Potters Bar finds itself in Hertfordshire and Barnet in London.

Middlesex is not immune from London's notorious traffic and parking problems so directions for the walks take into account that public transport will usually be the better way of reaching the starting points. Those walks which are not circular are best enjoyed with the help of a One Day Travelcard (available from LT and BR stations) which frees the traveller from the restrictions of normal return tickets.

For those who like to break their walk for refreshment the names of good pubs and places serving tea along or near the routes are mentioned.

The historical notes are designed to provide basic information about the places of interest along the route, and will be found at the end of each chapter. The very rough estimated time given for each walk is determined not just by distance but the terrain and number of viewpoints and historic buildings encountered.

The sketch map that accompanies each walk is designed to guide walkers to the starting point and give a simple yet accurate idea of the route to be taken. When appropriate, please remember the Country Code and make sure gates are not left open or any farm animals disturbed.

No special equipment is needed to enjoy the countryside on foot, but do wear a stout pair of shoes and remember that at least one muddy patch is likely even on the sunniest day.

Many hours of enjoyment have gone into preparing these walks. I hope that the reader will go out and enjoy them too.

Leigh Hatts
March 1990

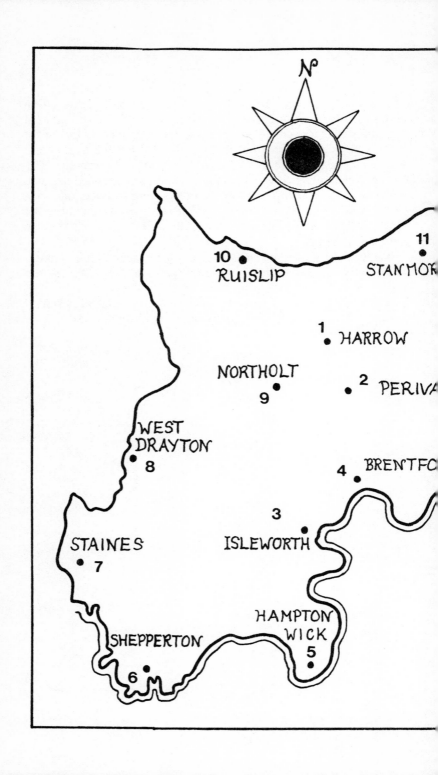

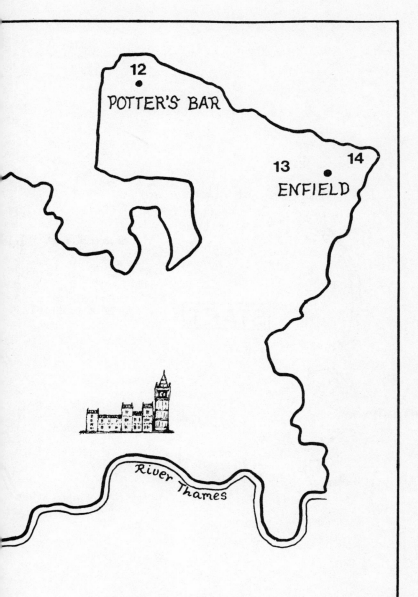

Sketch Map showing locations of the walks

Harrow on the Hill

playing fields

Northwick Park

START

South Kenton
BR & LT Station

Toll gate

Sudbury Hill BR
& LT Stations

Harrow

Introduction: Harrow on the Hill is one of the highest villages in Middlesex, the hill rising from the Middlesex plain to give sweeping views over the surrounding counties. The village itself is closely linked with Harrow school, and the extensive playing fields maintained by the school have helped to retain a rural atmosphere. This fascinating walk explores the historic heart of the village, with its Georgian houses and reminders of the famous people who have walked these streets over the centuries, and climbs to the beautiful parish church of St Mary on the crest of the hill. Here is the famous 'Peachey Stone', where Lord Byron would sit for hours and gaze out upon the landscape spread beneath him.

Distance: 2¼ miles which will take a leisurely 2 hours if time is spent enjoying the view from the church and exploring the village. But this is not a circular walk - the route ends at Sudbury Hill Underground station (Piccadilly line).

Refreshments: In Harrow there is the *Tea At Three* teashop (open daily except Wednesdays), the *Harrow Tuck Shop* and *The King's Head*.

How to get there: The walk starts at South Kenton Underground station (Bakerloo line) which is just east of the A404. There are no parking restrictions in the residential streets around the station.

The Walk: On descending from the South Kenton station platform turn left to join a short suburban road. At a junction go right into the north end of Nathans Road to enter Northwick Park.

Beyond the gate turn left to follow the edge of the park (left). Ahead can be seen the spire of Harrow church up on the hill. The path, barely visible in the grass, crosses a road and continues west. On approaching a belt of trees do not go ahead through the gap but turn right to follow the trees, which hide a stream.

On reaching a 'pitch & putt' course keep ahead towards Northwick Park hospital. Just before reaching the wire fence and car park, bear left to find the beginning of a path. The way, known as The Ducker Footpath, runs parallel to the hospital road (right) before swinging to the left and following a concrete wall (left) to a main road.

Cross Watford Road with care to climb over the wooden stile opposite and enter Harrow School playing field. Ahead is Harrow School and the village on the hill. Bear half-right towards the smaller (left-hand) spire on the school chapel. In season you will cross a couple of rugby pitches before passing under an oak tree where there is a gap in the fence. Keep forward towards the (incomplete) signpost at the top of a bank.

Walk through the double wooden gates (if locked go through the gap at the side) and up the steep Football Lane to reach the village. Turn left to cross the High Street on the zebra crossing. At once turn right along the pavement below the Speech Room. Where the road divides, a plaque records the first fatal road accident. Continue along the High Street (left fork) to pass a plaque on the left recalling Charles I's visit.

Just behond the Charles I plaque, and before the road runs down Grove Hill, turn left up a few steps to a narrow path where another plaque marks Sheridan's stables. Follow the path uphill to find Grove House on the right. Continue forward on the level for a few yards before taking the steps on the right up into the churchyard. Bear left and round the church to find the porch. The famous viewpoint of north Middlesex is to be found by Byron's 'Peachey Stone' just beyond the west end.

The walk leaves the churchyard by the lychgate. Continue down Church Hill, with views of the school chapel and the Vaughan Library on the left, to rejoin the High Street. Keep forward passing the Harrow School Bookshop on the left and the Harrow School Outfitters on the right. Except to visit the *Tea At Three* teashop, do not be tempted down West Street but stay on the higher level. Just beyond the Harrow Tuck Shop is the village square, dominated by the free-standing *King's Head* hotel sign showing Henry VIII.

Continue ahead along London Road, which contains interesting residences dating from the Georgian period. It is probably easiest to stay on the left-hand pavement before the road becomes a main road at the junction ahead. Follow the road round a double bend to go down Sudbury Hill - note The Orchard, built in 1900, on the second bend (right). Ahead is a good view down the hill. Before the next junction it would be helpful to be on the right-hand pavement.

At the junction with South Hill Avenue leave the main road by keeping ahead down a path known as Green Lane - a signpost points to 'Public Bridleway to Wood End Road'. The narrow path runs downhill to meet a road after ¼ mile. To the right is Orley Farm Road toll gate. Turn left along the road to reach *The Rising Sun*. Go right for Sudbury Hill BR station and, a little further on, Sudbury Hill Underground station (Piccadilly line).

Historical Notes

Harrow on the Hill: The landmark church was founded by Archbishop Lanfranc in 1087 and its spire was added in 1450. Among the brasses inside is one to John Lyon who founded Harrow School in 1572 with a charter from Elizabeth I - her statue can be seen outside the Speech Room. The other prominent spire belongs to the school chapel designed by George Gilbert Scott, who was also responsible for the Vaughan Library next door. Seven British prime ministers have been educated here including Peel (who lodged in what is now the School Bookshop) and Winston Churchill. The Harrow Tuck Shop has been in the same family for over 60 years.

Old Harrovian Richard Sheridan returned in 1871 to live at Grove House. As a pupil Byron spent many hours on the 'Peachey Stone' by the churchyard viewpoint which he recalled in Italy as his favourite spot. His daughter Allegra is buried under the church porch. The 18th century *King's Head* stands on the site of Henry VIII's hunting lodge. In 1646 Charles I had his last look at London as a free man from this hill, before he fled to the 'protection' of the Scots, who later gave him up to his Parliamentary enemies.

Orley Farm Road Toll Gate is a modern barrier but an old wooden gate is still maintained by South Hill Estates at the west end of South Hill Avenue. There the gate is usually locked to prevent any through traffic. When manned a toll of 30p per vehicle is levied. 'Orley Farm' recalls the novel of the same name written by Anthony Trollope, who lived nearby as a child.

Brent River Park

Introduction: The river Brent rises in Hertfordshire (where it is called the Dollis brook) and flows into the Thames at Brentford as the Grand Union Canal. In 1975 some 4½ miles of open land alongside the Brent between Hanger lane and Syon Park was created the 'Brent River Park', and so preserved an oasis of rural peace. This walk follows the river through the park from Perivale, which until the 1920s was still agricultural land, to Hanwell, with its Brunel viaduct. The contrast between the heavy traffic on the Western Avenue and the tranquillity of nearby Perivale churchyard is both surprising and refreshing.

Distance: 5½ miles, a circular walk which will take about 2½ hours. There is one short hill.

Refreshments: At Perivale there is *The Mylett Arms* and a café (in the nearby parade of shops, open weekday mornings until lunchtime). Refreshments are available in Brent Lodge Park opposite Hanwell church in the summer.

How to get there: Perivale is on Western Avenue (A40). It is possible to park near Perivale station at weekends or in Perivale Lane. Perivale Underground station is on the Piccadilly line.

The Walk: Turn left out of Perivale station to follow Horsenden Lane to Western Avenue, which must be crossed by the pedestrian bridge (right). From the bridge there is a view east to the nearby old Hoover factory.

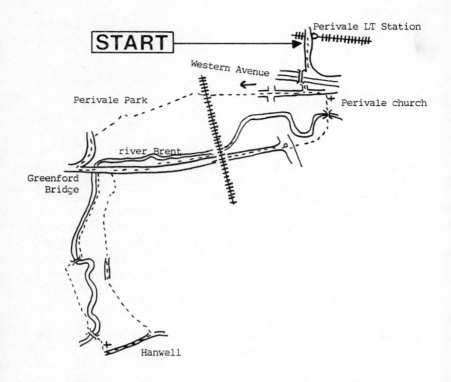

On the far side of the bridge at once turn away from the main road to follow Old Church Lane to a junction. Half-left under a chestnut tree is the lychgate entrance to Perivale church, where the walk will end. The outward route is to the right along Perivale Lane. In a gap in the hedge on the left can be seen the spire of St Stephen's, Drayton Green.

Keep ahead at the crossroads (with the Argyll Road extension) to follow Stockdove Way, which soon narrows to become a metalled footpath and cycleway. Pass under the railway bridge (carrying the link line between Ealing and the Perivale line) and bear right through Perivale Park's small car park. Beyond an iron gateway by a running track (right) bear left off the path and up a slight grassy slope. Follow a belt of trees on your left between a golf course and playing fields.

At the far end join a metalled path at a bend and keep forward. The path soon makes a double bend to cross a Brent tributary. At Costons Lane (once liable to flooding) cross over and turn left to walk round the corner, with a view of the ballustraded Greenford Bridge. Turn left into Ruislip Road to cross the fine bridge over the river Brent.

After a few yards turn right down some steps to find a gravelled riverside path. Follow this path downstream (with the river to the right). At first the riverside path is by a playing field but after a short distance the way runs below a high bank.

On approaching a footbridge there is a clear view of Hanwell church between the trees. Cross the bridge and at once bear left and left again onto an enclosed stony path. The way runs across the Brent Valley Golf Course before again becoming enclosed in a tunnel of trees. The path briefly touches the river before running ahead to Boles Bridge. Cross the footbridge and keep to the right of Boles Meadow (by Brent Lodge Park). The stepped path leads up to Hanwell church.

Do not go through the lychgate but turn left to pass the front (south side) of the church and follow Church Road along the top of Churchfields (right). After passing the thatched gothic cottage, go left by Madge Hill - a signpost points to Greenford and Perivale.

Go round the wooden gate and down the winding leafy path, known as High Lane but formerly 'Hay Lane'. At the bottom of the hill the way is metalled and, beyond a wooden gate, the lane briefly becomes a fully constructed road complete with pavement - an example of how the entire length of lane could have become but for such pressure groups as the Brent River & Canal Society. After 250 yards the lane meets an iron gate and immediately narrows into a gravelled footpath. The way ahead is below a low bank on the left, with a view behind of Hanwell church. After ¼ mile the path veers to the right to meet barriers.

On the far side do not go ahead towards the houses but turn left along a straight metalled path to continue in a northerly direction. At Ruislip Road turn right. Here you may prefer to use the left-hand pavement where, after the bus stop by the traffic lights, there is a parallel footpath up on the bank near the river. Before the railway bridge it is necessary to return to the road. Use the zebra crossing to go back to the right-hand pavement. Continue ahead to the roundabout at Argyll Road.

Go ahead over the road and directly forward on a metalled footpath. A signpost points to Perivale and Brentham. At the next 2 junctions keep left to reach a wooden bridge spanning the Brent. Ahead is Perivale church, on the path leading to a lychgate.

At the gate bear half-left to cross Perivale Lane and walk up Old Church Lane at the side of *The Mylett Arms*. Retrace the outward route over Western Avenue to Perivale station.

Historical Notes

Perivale means 'Pear Tree Valley', but the name has only been used since the Tudor period. Before the 16th century the village was known as 'Greenford Parva'. St Mary's church, dating from 1135, is mainly a 13th century building with a weatherboarded west tower added in 1510. The tiny building, declared redundant in 1972, was still a suitable size for the parish at the beginning of the 20th century, when the population was only 60. Occasional services, such as Harvest Festival, are still held.

The Great Western Railway station (the Underground since 1947) opened in 1904 as Perivale Halt, and the Western Avenue was cut through here in the 1920s. The famous Hoover factory, which is being converted into a superstore, was built in 1932. *The Mylett Arms*, on the site of Church Farm, is named after a local family commemorated by 16th century brasses in the church.

Hanwell: The sight of Hanwell church among the trees, from the railway viaduct, was appreciated by Queen Victoria on her journeys between London and Windsor. St Mary's, built in 1841, was the first church designed by George Gilbert Scott, but it stands on the site of a 12th century church. Buried in the crypt is Joseph Hanway, inventor of the umbrella. Past incumbents include Dr Sam Glass, George III's chaplain; Derwent Taylor Coleridge, the poet's son, and more recently Frederick Secombe, Sir Harry's brother.

The Brunel viaduct predates the present church by 4 years, but slightly older than both is Rectory Cottage opposite the church. Further along Church Road is The Hermitage, a thatched cottage with pointed windows which featured in the Prince of Wales' 'A Vision of Britain' exhibition at the Victoria & Albert Museum in 1989.

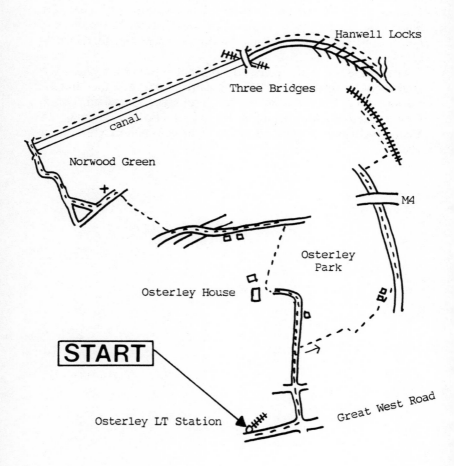

Hanwell Locks

Three Bridges

canal

Norwood Green

Osterley Park

M4

Osterley House

START

Osterley LT Station

Great West Road

Osterley

Introduction: Osterley Park is one of the treasured 'green lungs' of Outer London, given to the National Trust in 1949 by the Earl of Jersey. This exhilarating walk not only explores the park, with an opportunity to visit the beautiful mansion which was largely transformed by William Chambers and Robert Adam in the 18th century, but also the towpath alongside the Grand Union Canal. Here is Hanwell's 'staircase' of 6 locks, culminating in the famous Three Bridges. Norwood Green's charming village green, flanked by historic houses and its little church, is an additional attraction on this varied walk. You may be lucky enough to return home with some of the local produce which is on sale throughout the year at both Osterley and Norwood Green.

Distance: 6½ miles, a circular walk which will take about 2½ hours. The hill on the canal is a gentle climb. Note that one of the Osterley Park paths on this walk is closed from 8.00 pm, or sunset if earlier, until 10.00 am.

Refreshments: There is *The Fox* at the bottom of Hanwell Locks and 3 pubs at Norwood Green. The Osterley House café in the Tudor stables is open daily, noon to 5.30, March to October.

How to get there: The walk begins at Osterley park Underground station (Piccadilly line) on the Great West Road (A4).

The Walk: On leaving Osterley Underground station turn left along the Great West Road to the crossroads. Turn left by the post office up Thornbury Road. Janeve Bakery on the right is noted for its bread. Continue over the railway to pass the former Osterley station, now a bookshop.

Keep ahead to enter Osterley Park at the road junction. Beyond the lodge on the right, bear half-right to follow the footpath by the fence. After 250 yards turn right through an iron kissing gate to follow an enclosed path between fields. The spire of St Mary's, Osterley can be seen to the south. At a second gate, the path turns right and then left to follow the side of the park. Beyond a brick wall, the way runs on to Wyke Green.

Still keep forward to meet a driveway running up to the 2 Adam lodges - one white and the other pink. Continue across the drive and bear half-left towards *The Hare & Hounds* ahead. Over to the right is Osterley Garden Centre. On meeting Windmill Road, cross over to the pub and turn left to follow the pavement. The road runs downhill to pass under the M4.

Beyond the bridge a path runs down to a stream in Long Wood. Unfortunately this is not yet a through path so continue along the main road for 100 yards and turn right on to a narrow footpath. The way runs between Warren Farm playing fields on the left and a field with (usually) horses. At the far end do not go across the level crossing but turn left on another very narrow path between the playing field fence and the railway (right), the Brentford Docks branch line.

After ¼ mile the path turns right to an iron gate. Cross the railway with great care - the curving line does not allow for much visibility. Beyond the wooden stile opposite, bear half-left down the corner of an old hay meadow to the Grand Union Canal. Ahead is the confluence of the canal and the river Brent. Use the lock gates to cross the canal. (For *The Fox* cross the river Brent and turn left into pretty Green Lane.)

The walk continues, not over the Brent, but left up the 'staircase' of 6 locks. Soon the towpath passes the Fitzherbert Walk entrance on the right. Later the towpath curves to the west as it climbs 53ft. The fourth lock - number 94 - is known as Asylum Lock after the former Hanwell Asylum over the wall. Beyond the final

Hanwell lock, the towpath runs simultaneously over a railway and under a road, at a point known as Three Bridges.

Just after the next bridge, by Norwood Top Lock, there is a café (open weekday mornings). After a short distance the path rises and falls over the entrance to a canal arm built in 1913 for the Maypole margarine factory. After another ½ mile, climb up the ramp (with ridges to help the towing horses) to cross the road bridge and pass the waterside *Lamb* pub.

Keep ahead on the main road to pass *The Wolf* on the right, with its giant cricket bat on the outside wall, and Bridge View (right on the bend) where marmalade and jam are usually on sale for charity. Soon after a gentle double bend bear left along the side of Norwood Green. Continue ahead to pass The Grange and Friars Lawn, a pair of 18th century houses.

At the far end turn left into Tentelow Lane to pass the church on the left. Continue ahead, noting the charming Norwood Terrace on your right, to pass *The Plough*. Turn right by the pub's sign to follow an enclosed path. Go over a residential road and between 2 gardens to a field.

On the far side of the field join Osterley Lane to go over the M4, where you will find a good view of the walled Osterley Park Farm. Where the lane meets a junction do not go between the lodges but keep ahead through the white iron gate where the way becomes rougher.

After 325 yards turn right by a lonely, empty lodge to a gateway. Use the small gate to enter Osterley Park. Keep on the gravel path and soon there is a view of Osterley House ahead. At a junction of paths bear right only for the house, toilets and the café in the stables.

The walk continues to the left on the metalled path, which at once curves to the south to run along the edge of the lake. Keep ahead to pass a house on the left selling farm produce. Continue along the drive to the main gateway and retrace the outward route to the station.

Historical Notes

Osterley Station: The original station, called 'Osterley & Spring Grove', opened in 1883 in Thornbury Road and was succeeded by the present one, designed by Charles Holden and on a new site, in 1934. The old station building survives as the popular Osterley Bookshop, specialising in second-hand books.

Osterley: Sir Thomas Gresham, founder of Gresham College and the Royal Exchange, built the present house just in time for Elizabeth I's visit in 1576. It was the banker Francis Child in the 18th century who called in William Chambers to alter the west front and Robert Adam to transform the east front with an entrance based on Rome's Portico of Septimus Serverus. The interior was considered to be as lavish as a palace even in the 18th century, when the house was already open to visitors. Early in the 19th century the property passed to the 5th Earl of Jersey and the 9th and present Earl gave the house and grounds to the National Trust in 1949. The house is open Tuesdays to Sundays, and there is an admission fee.

The Grand Union Canal was opened in 1794. South from the Hanwell locks it follows the canalised river Brent to join the Thames at the former Brentford Docks. This is the 'main line' to Birmingham via Uxbridge.

Fitzherbert Walk was opened in 1983 to create a link between the canal and Hanwell by way of the bank of the non-navigable river Brent. It is named after Luke Fitzherbert, founder of the Brent River & Canal Society, who conceived the idea of the Brent River Park. The Fitzherbert Walk is a vital link in the River Park.

Hanwell Locks: The flight of 6 locks raises the canal by 53 ft in a ⅓ mile. A boat takes about 1½ hours to pass through. The high brick wall hides St Bernard's Hospital - the former Hanwell Asylum built in 1831 and housing 2,000 inmates by the turn of the century. Its coal arrived by barge and Lock 94 is known as Asylum Lock. The Hanwell locks feature in AP Herbert's *The Water Gypsies*.

Three Bridges is really 'two bridges' but remains a unique Middlesex feature. At this point the canal is simultaneously above a railway line and below a road. The Southall-Brentford Docks branch line was built in 1859 and passes underneath in a tunnel designed by Isambard Kingdom Brunel.

Norwood Green: St Mary's church was heavily restored in 1864 but the walls date from the 12th century. The village maintains its community feeling, although the annual cricket match between *The Lamb* and *The Wolf* ceased in 1963 due to lack of younger players. The pub matches are commemorated by the huge bat outside *The Wolf*. Bridge View, near *The Wolf*, regularly sells homemade marmalade and jam in aid of Cancer Research.

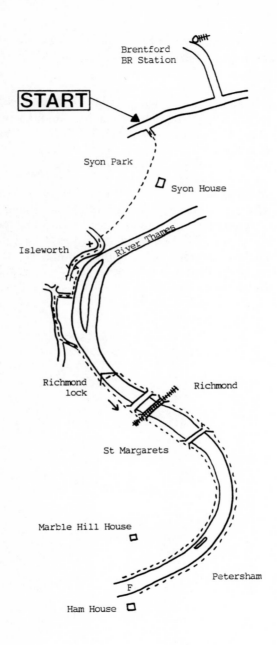

Brentford
BR Station

START

Syon Park

Syon House

River Thames

Isleworth

Richmond
lock

Richmond

St Margarets

Marble Hill House

Petersham

F

Ham House

Isleworth

Introduction: The heart of old Isleworth lies by the river Thames and this beautiful walk follows the river from Brentford, the old county town of Middlesex, to Richmond. Until recently such a walk would have had to be along the Surrey side, but the opening of more paths along the 'north' bank has opened up the Isleworth section of the river. From Syon Park, and magnificent Syon House, the route takes you down to the river at Isleworth. Following the Thames, past Richmond Lock and Richmond Bridge, the grounds of Marble Hill are reached, with the lovely 18th century villa and wonderful views across the Thames. Taking the ferry across the river, the return journey commences by passing close by Ham House, and recrosses the river by Richmond Lock.

Distance: 7 miles, a circular walk which will take about 2½ hours. There are no hills.

Refreshments: There are teashops at Syon House (by the footpath), Marble Hill House and Ham House. There are 2 pubs on the Richmond towpath as well as fast food restaurants in the town.

How to get there: Brentford and Syon are on the A315. Parking in Brentford is limited but the Syon House car park is open free to those visiting the house or an attraction during the walk. Syon Park is a short step from Brentford station on the Waterloo-Kingston line.

The Walk: The walk begins just beyond the west end of Brentford High Street at the first bus stop in London Road. From Brentford station walk south down Boston Manor Road and turn right into the High Street. Turn south (left), opposite Field Lane, down a short road leading to a Syon Park gateway.

Beyond the gate, by Brent Lea Recreation Ground (right), follow the walled footpath which curves to the right to emerge by buildings. Keep ahead, passing the café and National Trust shop on the left, and just past the St Richard Reynolds blue plaque (left above the arch) the path moves out to skirt the building ahead. Still keep forward on the main drive, ignoring a footpath branching left. Soon there is a fine view to the left of Syon House. Follow the drive for just over ¼ mile to a main gateway by a lodge.

Turn left past The Ferry House to the river at Isleworth. If the road is flooded use the raised path in front of the church where past flood levels are recorded. Continue on the road past *The London Apprentice* on the left and Richard Reynolds House on the right.

Before the bridge ahead, turn left under the arch of Bridge Wharf Road. At once go right, up a short narrow passage to follow the side of the Duke of Northumberland's River. Cross the footbridge over the mouth to rejoin the Thames by a remaining riverside crane. The new path, with a view across the water to Isleworth Ait, which is part of Middlesex, runs ahead and across *The Town Wharf* pub terrace.

Cross the top of the steep slipway and continue upstream for a few yards. But on meeting the end of a lane - Lion Wharf - do not be tempted through the gap in the wall ahead on to a new landscaped riverside path. At present it has no southern exit. Instead turn right, up the lane and away from the river to pass the entrance to Herons Place on the left. At a junction by *The Castle* turn left along the main road to pass the entrance to Nazareth House, a home for the aged run by the Poor Sisters of Nazareth.

Keep by the high wall and stay on the main road to cross the river Crane. At once turn left into the walled Railshead Road to rejoin the Thames. Isleworth Promenade runs in front of the former

Maria Grey College. Where the way divides keep on the narrow riverside path to join Ranelagh Drive. Continue past Richmond Lock and, where the road swings away, stay with the river to go under Twickenham Bridge and Richmond Railway Bridge.

The path runs ahead as Ducks Walk, with the river hidden behind gardens. After briefly joining a road and passing a chandlery, the path continues. At the far end the way becomes a road and reaches Willoughby House on the right, with its tall tower dating from the 1820s, in St Margaret's.

Use the crossing on the approach to Richmond Bridge and turn left down to the river to find the riverside path. Cars parked here are often caught by the rising tide. Across the river *The Captain Webb* floating hotel may be at her mooring. As the path bends there is a view up to the Star and Garter Home on Richmond Hill and below, across Petersham Meadows, can be seen the 'new' (or Victorian) Petersham church. Glover's island is considered part of Middlesex. The path runs the length of the Marble Hill grounds. At the far end is Hammerton's Ferry, which operates daily 10.00am to 6.00pm (6.30 weekends). Cross the Thames on the ferry to reach the towpath on the Surrey side.

On the 'south' bank climb the landing steps and, except to visit Ham House, do not go ahead but turn left to walk downstream.

The towpath crosses the end of River Lane, leading to Petersham village, before following the riverside edge of Petersham Meadows, which has the nearest herd of cows to Trafalgar Square.

The path, although still the towpath, runs a little inland for a short distance before returning to the river at *The Three Pigeons* on the edge of Richmond. Stay on the metalled path to pass *The Captain Webb's* mooring and under Richmond Bridge.

Beyond the classical Quinlan Terry development on the right, the path runs across the Water Lane draw dock by *The White Cross*. From here the towpath is known as Cholmondeley Walk as it passes the site of Richmond Palace. Beyond the 18th century cottages by Friars Lane there is a view of Trumpeter's House (right) which replaced the palace's middle gateway.

Pass under Richmond Railway Bridge and Twickenham Bridge to reach Richmond Lock. Climb the steps to cross the river and retrace the outward route to Syon.

Historical Notes

Syon House was a Bridgettine convent from 1431 until Henry VIII closed it in 1534. The 60 sisters and 25 priests and brothers were headed by an abbess. One of the priests was St Richard Reynolds, who was executed at Tyburn for refusing to take the Oath of Supremacy acknowledging Henry as head of the church. The community, which moved to the safety of Portugal, is now in Devon. On his death, King Henry's body rested here on its way to Windsor. Elizabeth I gave the buildings to the Earl of Northumberland, whose distant successor, the Duke of Northumberland, now lives here in a house transformed by Robert Adam in the 1760s. Visitors have included Guy Fawkes on 4th November 1605 and Charles I, who called on his children just before his confinement and execution. The Great Conservatory in the grounds is said to have inspired Paxton's Crystal Palace. Among other attractions today is a wholefood shop in the monastic barn, a butterfly museum and the gardens, which are open all year. The house is open afternoons, Sunday to Thursday from Easter to September, and there is an admission fee.

Isleworth: The name has evolved from the 7th century 'Gislheresuuyrth' meaning 'Gislhere's homestead'. The modern church retains its 15th century tower. The artists Turner and Van Gogh both briefly lived in the village. *The London Apprentice* is named after the livery company apprentices who used to row up the river from the City on their annual day's holiday. There was a ferry here from Henry VIII's reign until 1960, with a brief restoration in 1983.

Duke of Northumberland's River is an artificial waterway dug during Henry VII's reign to bring water from the nearby river Crane to the mill at Syon Abbey. The river was named after the Duke in the 18th century.

Marble Hill House, designed by amateur architect Lord Herbert, was completed in 1729 for Henrietta Howard, mistress of the future George II. The white and gold Great Room is modelled on Inigo Jones' single cube room at Wilton House. Henrietta lived here until her death in 1769, having become firm friends with her neighbours Alexander Pope and Horace Walpole. The recent restoration of Marble Hill has been said to be 'as important and successful as the restoration of the Grand Trianon at Versailles'. The black walnut tree near the river gate is the largest in the country, having been planted at about the same time that the house was built. The house can be visited daily except Fridays; free.

Richmond was 'West Sheen' until Henry VII named his new palace here 'Richmond' after one of his titles derived from Yorkshire. Although a London Borough since 1965, the town retains its Surrey country-town atmosphere. Its most outstanding landmark is the neo-classical 1980s development of shops and offices on the riverside by Quinlan Terry.

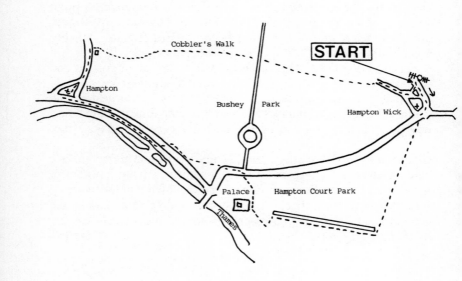

Hampton Court

Introduction: Cardinal Wolsey's magnificent Hampton Court Palace, its park bordered by the Thames, is one of the most famous landmarks of Middlesex. This tranquil walk takes you through the Park, where deer and sheep roam freely and the water birds of the Long Water are an added attraction, towards the Palace itself. Joining a Thames riverside path, it passes Tagg's Island and Garrick's Temple, and leads on to Hampton church, with its panoramic view of the Thames and Hampton Ferry. Beautiful Bushey Park, the Cobblers Walk through open countryside with views of 18th century Bushey House, and the Chestnut Avenue planted for William III, end this delightful ramble.

Distance: 5½ miles, a circular walk which will take about 2½ hours. There are no hills.

Refreshments: There is a pub, *The Old King's Head*, at the start of the walk and a café in Hampton Court Palace. The *Palace Tea Rooms*, opposite the main gates, is open daily until 8.00 pm.

How to get there: Hampton Wick is on the A310. Parking is available in some side streets and in Kingston-upon-Thames over Kingston Bridge. Hampton Wick station is on the Waterloo-Shepperton-Feltham line.

The Walk: Turn left out of Hampton Wick station and walk along the High Street to the roundabout at the Kingston Bridge approach. Keep forward to *The Old King's Head* on the left, where there is an entrance to Hampton Court Park.

Go through the park gateway and follow the metalled road over the cattle grid and up the hill. There is a view of Hampton Wick Pond to the right. Keep right where the road divides and soon there is a view (half-right) of Hampton Court Palace a mile away.

At the second fork bear left. Over to the left can be seen the campanile of St Raphael's on the far bank of the Thames. After nearly ½ mile, just before the cattle grid, bear half-right up to a wooden stile at the corner of the Long Water. With the water to your right, walk towards the Palace ahead. At the far end bear half-left with an iron fence to find a large ornamental iron gateway. Go through the small gate on the left and cross the canal footbridge.

Walk ahead through the formal gardens towards the east front of the Palace. At the Palace turn right along the Broad Walk. Beyond the Royal Tennis Court on your left, turn left through a small gateway and at once bear half-right (where a sign points to the Maze) to walk through The Wilderness to the Lion Gate.

At the road, turn left past *The King's Arms* and before the bend ahead cross the road. Walking on the right-hand pavement, go ahead at the bend through a gap in the fence on to the green. Continue ahead on an almost invisible path, which becomes well defined before reaching the green's opposite corner.

At the main road turn right. Soon the pavement becomes raised as it runs alongside the edge of Bushey Park to the right. Just beyond the Swiss chalet on the left, cross the road to follow a riverside path by the Thames. Soon after the bridge leading on to Tagg's Island, the way narrows to cross a stream. When the path runs up to the road, turn left along the pavement. When level with Garrick's Villa (on your right with a blue plaque) return to the riverside to pass Garrick's Temple.

On returning again to the road, beyond the Temple, cross the road and turn left to visit Hampton church, where there is a panoramic view of the Thames and Hampton Ferry below. Follow the path round the east end of the church to join the High Street. Walk on the right-hand pavement for nearly ½ mile to *The Duke's Head*. Turn down the far side of the pub to find a gate leading into Bushey Park and the start of Cobbler's Walk.

The enclosed metalled path runs for ¼ mile to the Longford river. Cross the wooden bridge. After the river swings north the way leads to a wooden gate. Keep forward on a metalled path. After 250 yards go ahead whilst the metalled path swings half-left. Cobbler's Walk is now a narrow rough path over flat open country. Later there is a view on the left of Bushey House, before the path runs parallel with a park road to the left just after a junction.

At the major junction ahead, cross the raised Chestnut Avenue. The footpath is now metalled. At once take the left fork, which runs through bracken before reaching the Leg of Mutton Pond on the right. Soon after crossing a stream, the path reaches Hampton Wick Gate. Outside there is a notice recalling cobbler Timothy Bennett and a memorial to him.

Turn right along the road and (unless returning to Kingston) keep ahead and to the left where the road divides. Turn left into School Road and left again at the High Street to reach Hampton Wick station.

Historical Notes

Hampton Wick was a hamlet of Hampton, 2 miles away. The hamlet only built its own church when Hampton was rebuilding its ancient church in the 1820s. E. Lapidge was architect for both churches.

Hampton Court Park, also known as Home Park, was first enclosed by Henry VIII. Charles I rode here in the autumn of 1647 when being held prisoner at the Palace by Cromwell. One day he made a briefly successful bid for freedom when he rode out of the gates and made for the south coast. Later his son, Charles II, had the ¾ mile Long Water dug. This straight canal attracts moorhens and often cormorants are seen here. The avenues of trees also date back to the 17th century. Deer and sheep still roam the park.

Hampton Court Palace was a house of the Knights Hospitallers, rebuilt by Cardinal Wolsey to such a size that it needed almost 500 servants. He presented the residence to Henry VIII, who brought 5 of his 6 wives here. He is said to have been playing in the tennis court when he received confirmation of Anne Boleyn's execution at the Tower of London. Elizabeth I usually passed Christmas here and enjoyed gardening. The Vine was planted in 1768 by 'Capability' Brown for George III, who declined to live here on the grounds that he remembered having his ears boxed in the State Rooms by his grandfather. William IV started guided tours and Queen Victoria opened the main rooms in 1838 for free public viewing. There is now an admission charge, and the Palace is open daily.

Hampton Court Green: On the south side, near the Royal Mews, there is The Old Court House where Sir Christopher Wren lived from 1706 until his death in 1723. Faraday House was the retirement home of Michael Faraday, the discoverer of electricity, from 1858 to 1867.

Tagg's Island, named after Royal Waterman Tom Tagg, is part of Middlesex. Earlier this century the island was famous as Fred Karno's leisure complex. The Swiss chalet by the river's north bank was brought here from Switzerland in 1899.

Hampton is well known for its waterworks to the west. There has been a riverside church here since at least 1342. The present church by E. Lapidge was completed in 1831. A recent parishioner until his death in 1983 was Eric Fraser, who invented 'Mr Therm' and drew for *The Radio Times*. His designs decorate an interior door. Garrick's Temple, by the river, was built in 1765 for actor Richard Garrick who lived across the road. *The Bull*, rebuilt in 1893, has been on the same site since Henry VIII's reign, when the ferry service started.

Bushey Park is, like Hampton Court Park, a deer park enclosed by Henry VIII. Charles I had the Longford river dug in 1639 to bring water from the river Colne near Longford to feed the ponds. Wren was responsible for the Chestnut Avenue planted for William III as a grand approach to Hampton Court Palace. Near the Avenue's south end is the statue of Diana carved by Fanelli for Charles I and moved to its present position as part of Christopher Wren's plans for an English rival to Versailles. The early 18th century Bushey House was home to Lord North during his premiership, and to William IV before he became King - he lived there with actress Dorothy Jordan and their 10 children. It is now part of the National Physical Laboratory.

Cobbler's Walk is a public footpath in Bushey Park. In 1754 it was saved by Hampton Wick cobbler Timothy Bennett, who had noticed that people no longer passed his shop on their way to Kingston Market. Bennett's willingness to go to law to keep the short cut open resulted in Bushey Park Ranger Lord Halifax reopening the path.

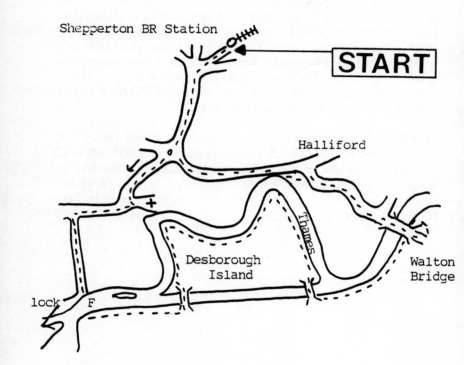

Shepperton BR Station

START

Halliford

Thames

Desborough
Island

Walton
Bridge

lock   F

Shepperton

Introduction: Shepperton was best known in the past for its film studios, but this attractive Thames-side village is worth exploring in its own right. This walk from Shepperton follows the boundaries of old Middlesex, with the help of an ancient ferry crossing.

At Shepperton Lock ring for the ferryman, and enjoy the sight of the colourful river traffic which keeps this lock busy, before continuing the walk on the Surrey side of the river past D'Oyly Carte island. The route returns to Shepperton through peaceful woodland and along the towpath. On the way it passes through Lower Halliford, another village which has kept its rural atmosphere and which was once popular with poets and writers.

Distance: 4¾ miles, a circular walk which will take about 2¼ hours depending on the ferry, which runs hourly. There are no hills but 2 flights of steps.

Refreshments: There are pubs in Shepperton's Church Square and (in season) a tea stall at Shepperton Lock.

How to get there: Shepperton is on the A244 and near junction 1 on the M3. There is a car park on the route in Church Road just beyond the new roundabout at the south end of the High Street. The easiest way to reach Shepperton is by train. Shepperton station is a railhead served by trains from Waterloo.

The Walk: From the station go down Station Approach to the crossroads and turn left into the High Street. At the far end, where the war memorial now stands on a new roundabout, go ahead to follow Church Road and pass the car park on the left.

(For an early glimpse of the river Thames and a view of Desborough Island, turn left through the car park and follow a path by a high brick wall.)

Church Road leads into Church Square, the picturesque village centre. Ferry Square, beyond the church, should be explored for its fine river view.

The walk continues along Chertsey Road. Turn left into Ferry Lane, which leads directly to the ferry near Shepperton Lock.

Ring the bell at the appointed hour on the ferry notice to call the ferryman and cross to the Surrey bank. (If you have to wait you can sit on the seats at the nearby Shepperton Lock - one of the busiest on the river. The tea stall on the lock island is just in Middlesex.)

On landing on the Surrey bank, turn left to walk downstream along the towpath. Level with D'Oyly Carte Island can be seen the lychgate, complete with bell for calling a boat from the island before the footbridge was erected. Soon the river divides into the Old Thames and the straight Desborough Cut. Climb the steps ahead to walk over the cut and on to Desborough Island.

Where the road swings away, keep forward through a (probably broken) gateway to a path which runs down to bear right on to the riverbank. This is the old towpath and almost at once there is a view ahead of Shepperton Manor. After 300 yards the village comes into view and a notice on the right marks Point Meadow. In the bushes there is a rusty 1861 City Post.

As the path turns east it runs a little away from the bank. A lone iron boundary marker indicates the limit of Thames Conservancy-owned land. The towpath now runs north and then south through woodland with occasional river views for the next ½ mile. At a drive, by a lodge on the right, keep ahead to join a road which swings in from the right. Continue forward uphill to leave the island by a high bridge crossing the Cut.

On the far side, at once go left down a flight of steps. The towpath runs ahead on to the flat flood plain of Cowey Sale which is part of Middlesex. Do not attempt to join the approach road to the ugly Walton Bridge but stay on the riverbank and walk underneath. At once follow a metalled path running inland to find a flight of steps. Climb up on to the road to walk over the bridge.

Once on the 'north' bank continue down to a road junction to cross the main flow of traffic and walk up Walton Lane. Follow this partly rural road for nearly ½ mile to reach the green at Lower Halliford. On the left is a blue Middlesex County plaque on the home of poet and author Thomas Love Peacock (1832-1866).

The footpath cuts the corner to give a view of the river which Peacock would have known. Turn left at the road, which runs close to the water but has a very narrow pavement on the left-hand side. Stay on the road (but use the right-hand pavement) to pass 3 pubs - *The Red Lion*, *The Ship* and *The Crown*. At the roundabout, turn right for Shepperton station or left for the car park.

Historical Notes:

County Boundaries: The main channel of the river Thames is usually accepted as the southern boundary of Middlesex. Any islands north of the navigation channel are therefore usually within the old county. An exception is at Shepperton, where the large Desborough Island falls within old Surrey and the old course of the river remains the boundary. However the riverside around the southern end of Walton Bridge falls within Middlesex rather than Surrey - a fact still recognised by district council boundaries.

Shepperton means 'shepherds' habitation' and according to the Domesday Book, it belonged to Westminster Abbey. Its church was destroyed by flooding during the 1605-6 winter when the Thames was still tidal here. The present church, dedicated to St Nicholas (patron of sailors), was built in 1614, with the tower added during the next century.

Behind the church is the rectory, which dates from the very early 15th century although the front is Queen Anne period. It was there in the 1840s that hymn writer JM Neale, author of *Good King Wenceslas*, wrote his novel *Shepperton Manor*. At the 9 bedroom Manor House, George Eliot wrote *Scenes from Clerical Life*.

Charles Dickens visited the village and much later his *Oliver Twist* was filmed at nearby Shepperton Studios, which opened in 1928. Willow trees here inspired the *Mikado* song, *Tit-willow*.

Shepperton Ferry reopened in 1986 after a 26 year break. There had been a ferry here since Henry VI's reign. In the 18th century it cost one shilling to take a drove of oxen across on the way to Kingston market. Between the two World Wars, when Sid Kingman was ferryman for 22 years, the fare was 1d (or 2d if you had a bicycle) and the ferry operated daily from 6.00 am to 10.00 pm. Today the service is at least every hour between 8.00 am and 5.00 pm with a final run at 5.30. Cycles are carried at half price.

D'Oyly Carte Island, once known as Silly Island, belongs to the Surrey side. The building was intended as a summer annexe to the *Savoy* hotel. Visitors included William S. Gilbert and Arthur Sullivan.

Desborough Island was created when the Cut was dug in the early 1930s after years of complaints from barge operators about the 5 tortuous bends at Shepperton. The ¾ mile channel was opened by Lord Desborough, chairman of the Thames Conservancy Board, in 1935.

City Posts were erected in 1861 to coincide with the Metropolitan Police boundary. In 1694 the City was allowed to levy a tax on coal and wine coming into London by boat. The money raised after 1861 was used to free nearby Walton Bridge and 4 others from tolls.

Cowey Sale, meaning 'cow way', is a low lying meadow which may have once been part of the Thames bed. The Engine river, to the south, is said to have been an alternative channel for the Thames and the whole area is still liable to flooding.

The Engine river, marking the old Middlesex-Surrey boundary, is still the boundary between Spelthorne and Elmbridge District Councils.

Lower Halliwell: Thomas Love Peacock bought the riverside Peacock House at the start of Walton Lane for his mother in 1826. He lived there permanently until his death in 1866. His son-in-law George Meredith lived at Vine Cottage across the green.

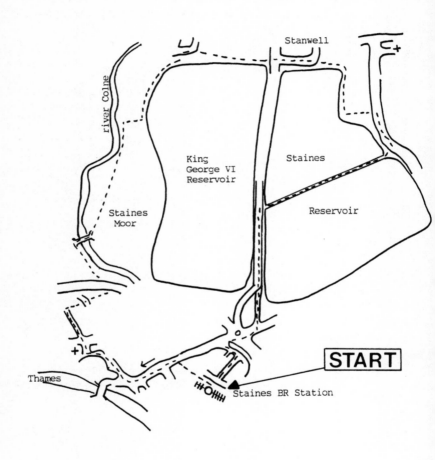

Staines and Stanwell

Introduction: The ancient riverside town of Staines is the starting point for the unusual walk. The countryside between Staines and Stanwell is flat moorland, a reminder that this area was part of Hounslow Heath, once notorious for its highwaymen and wild isolation. Staines Moor is now a Site of Special Scientific Interest, and the area is popular with birdwatchers. Canada Geese are often to be seen flying over the moor, and enormous numbers of water birds, particularly gulls, congregate on the huge expanse of Staines reservoir.

When the reservoir was built, the villagers of Stanwell insisted on being provided with a path across it so that they could still walk to Staines. Your return route traces that path between the 2 enormous lakes. Being above ground level, there are views from here across to Heathrow, the North Downs and Windsor Great Park. The reservoir is now just inside the 40 square mile Colne Valley Park, which extends northwards as far as Rickmansworth in Hertfordshire.

Distance: 5½ miles, a circular walk which will take about 2½ hours. There are no hills although the reservoir path is above ground level.

Refreshments: Staines has plenty of pubs and fast food restaurants. There are 3 pubs in Stanwell, as well as the village shop.

How to get there: Staines is on the A30 just off the M25. Parking can be difficult although there is sometimes space near the church. The town is well served by trains on the Waterloo-Reading line.

The Walk: The starting point is Staines High Street. Leave Staines station by the 'up' platform and at once turn left to follow Station Path, which leads directly to the High Street. Turn left at the main road to walk under the railway bridge and along the High Street.

At the western end of the High Street, by the Market Square, bear half-right into Church Street. Cross the river Colne and keep ahead at the junction to pass the town's former brewery building on the left. Follow the Georgian street to *The Bells* and turn right by the church up Vicarage Road. (The gateway just before the main road leads to the Royal Nanny's Tomb. Go right and left to find the grave at the end of the path before the round flowerbed.)

Cross the main road and continue ahead. At the far end, by the entrance to Moor House, turn right along a narrow metalled path which curves round to Moor Lane. But just before the end go directly ahead over the lane and through a gap by a green iron gate. A path runs uphill to cross the railway and then down to a kissing gate.

Beyond the gate go left under the Staines bypass to go through a wooden kissing gate on to Staines Moor. Bear half-left past a wooden fence corner towards a pylon. Keep to the right of the pylon to find the path beside the river Colne. After a short distance the path crosses the river by a concrete bridge.

Keep forward on the slightly winding path but when the way divides take the right fork. After a ¼ mile, where the path again divides, keep ahead on the right fork to find a plank bridge at a point known as Bone Head. (If you reach a second concrete bridge by a signpost, you should turn right to walk upstream.)

On the far side of the footbridge it may still be necessary to climb over a fallen tree. The way ahead is now enclosed to pass a gravel works on the right below the bank of the King George VI reservoir. The path may pass over a conveyor before crossing a lorry track at kissing gates. The way soon curves to the right to join another path at a long-broken stile.

Go left along the metalled path which runs by a high wire fence below the reservoir. At the end the path bears east by houses on Stanwell Moor. Later the path suddenly turns left to cross a concrete bridge over a stream and meets a road. Go right, and when the road turns north, keep ahead on to a track. Beyond the stream there is soon a view into the stables on the left. Soon, where the way ceases to be a bridlepath, there is a concrete surface.

At the main road cross over (there are traffic lights) to walk up Park Road opposite. Where the road bends left, cross with care to continue ahead up a narrow enclosed path. There are sometimes cattle in the long field on the right below the Staines reservoir. The path runs between private gardens and Thames Water land. After turning south there is a gate on the left leading into Stanwell's recreation ground.

(To visit the village cross the grass to the road and turn left along Town Lane. Ahead is *The Wheatsheaf* pub. The church is to the right, before the pub, at the end of Knyvett Close where a path leads to the village green and shops. The main walk can be joined again either at the recreation ground or further south in Town Lane.)

Beyond the recreation ground the path is less well maintained as it runs past the backs of the newer houses before turning east alongside the hedge hiding the cemetery.

At Town Lane go right along the wide grass verge. Beyond a double bend by allotments on the right, go through a kissing gate by a larger gateway to follow a path up the side of the reservoir. At the top, the path bears right to run between the 2 huge man-made lakes which make up Staines reservoir. This path replaces a direct route between Stanwell and Staines lost when the reservoir was built at the turn of the century.

Behind can be seen Heathrow Airport, whilst to the south (left) there are the North Downs. Ahead is Windsor Great Park. The wooded hill to the south-west is Cooper's Hill above Runnymede. At the far end of this ½ mile long path, popular with bird-watchers, the way turns left to run downhill to a kissing gate at the main road. Turn left to follow an inadequate pavement which, after ½ mile, leaves the main road to run ahead into quiet Stanwell New Road.

At the far end cross the main London Road and turn right to reach the Crooked Billet roundabout. Go ahead across the end of Staines bypass (there is a bridge) and turn right to follow the pavement round the corner. The main road ahead leads into Staines High Street. (To reach the station turn left by the bus garage into Greenlands Road and right into Rosefield Road. The station is ahead between 2 pubs.)

Historical Notes

Staines: It was from here that the Barons rode out to Runnymede to receive King John's assent to Magna Carta in 1215. It has been suggested that John lodged the night in a house which stood in Moor Lane. The Barons and the King would have forded the Thames, which did not have a bridge at this point until 7 years later. Staines Bridge has been rebuilt at least 5 times and the present structure, slightly upstream of its predecessors, was completed in 1832 to John Rennie's design. The Town Hall stands on the site of the market hall where Sir Walter Raleigh was found guilty of treason in 1603, when an outbreak of the plague forced the trial out of London. The church is early 19th century but has a brick tower dating from 1631. In the churchyard there is the tomb of Augusta Maria Byng, governess to the Kaiser's children. But the most famous landmark is not the church but Ashley's Brewery tower, built in 1903 and now converted into residential use as part of the Maltings development.

Staines Moor, just inside the Colne Valley Park, is a Site of Special Scientific Interest noted for its rare earthworms. Flocks of Canada Geese can often be seen flying here below the constant flow of aircraft using Heathrow Airport.

Stanwell: The church has a 14th century spire which leans to the south - the oak dried out more quickly on one side. Another oddity is in the churchyard, where a tombstone carries the date '31 February 1756'. In the church there is the tomb of Lord Knyvett, who arrested Guy Fawkes and who played host to Princess Elizabeth after James I declared that he wanted his daughter 'to breathe the sweet air of Middlesex'. The fine Lord Knyvett School, built with money left in his will, still stands at the east end of the High Street.

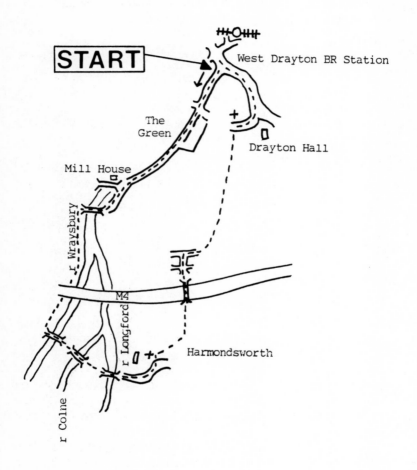

START

West Drayton BR Station

The Green

Drayton Hall

Mill House

r Wraysbury

M4

r Longford

Harmondsworth

r Colne

West Drayton

Introduction: West Drayton's green, the heart of the old village, is the setting for an attractive array of 18th and 19th century buildings. This gentle ramble passes close by Mill House, the Colne rushing beneath the old waterwheel, and then becomes a riverside walk, along the banks of the Wraysbury and the Colne. The destination is the finest medieval tithe barn in Middlesex, at Harmondsworth. Despite the proximity of Heathrow, Harmondsworth is still surrounded by green fields, and the return route is along a footpath which has been in use since Roman times.

Distance: 4 miles, a circular walk which will take about 1½ hours. There are no hills.

Refreshments: There are pubs in West Drayton and an attractive pub and village shop opposite Harmondsworth church.

How to get there: West Drayton is on the A408 and M4. Parking can be difficult on the main road and near the station on weekdays. West Drayton station is on the Paddington-Slough line.

The Walk: The starting point is Station Road. Leave the station by the 'down' side at the end of the tunnel below the platforms. Walk ahead and turn right and then left to reach the main road - Station Road.

Turn left into Station Road and go right by the post office into Swan Road. Keep ahead to pass through the heart of West Drayton - the Green. The road changes its name to Mill Road before passing the entrance to St George's Meadows on the left, a National Trust property (not open to the public). A little further on (also on the left) is the early 19th century Colne Mead, once the home of the father of actor and cricketer Sir Aubrey Smith.

Where the main road bears right over the bridge to Mill House, keep ahead, avoiding the bridge to pass *The Anglers' Retreat* on the left and the cricket ground known to Sir Aubrey. The road - Cricketfield Road - runs close to Fray's river before turning right to cross the water at the confluence of Fray's river and the river Colne.

On the far side turn left with the road, which enjoys various surfaces. After 250 yards the river again divides, but this time into the Colne and the river Wraysbury. Continue by the Wraysbury, and where the road ends keep ahead to go under the M4. To the right there is a view up to the M25 interchange on the Buckinghamshire border. Beyond the bridge, the riverside footpath is protected from the M25 traffic noise by a new high bank of earth on the right. Do not be tempted over the stepping stones, but cross the river on reaching a wide bridge with a parallel footbridge leading into Moor Lane. At a second bridge the lane crosses the river Colne.

Where the traffic turns down Accommodation Lane, keep forward between the posts. Soon the road rises to cross the Longford river, but just before there is a view (half-left) of Harmondsworth's church and great barn. Beyond the bridge, the lane curves round to enter the village.

At the green turn left to pass *The Five Bells* and go through the church gates. The public footpath is ahead, which passes the tombs of Peggy Bedford and Richard Cox on the left. At a junction go right to follow a narrow metalled path to the far corner of the churchyard. Walk between the brick gateposts to follow a well established footpath (once a Roman track to Staines) along the side of a field. Soon the path runs across open ground towards the M4, which is crossed by a bridge.

On the far side of the motorway continue northwards over a crossroads in a housing estate. At a T-junction turn right and after a short distance go left on to a signposted footpath by grass. The metalled path runs over the end of Wise Lane and ahead for over ½ mile to West Drayton church. Until 1975 this straight path approached the church along an avenue of elms.

At Church Road cross over to the old gatehouse by the church and turn right. Ignore the first turning and bear left with the road to pass Drayton Hall (to the right, in the trees) and reach Station Road. Turn left to return to the start of the walk.

Historical Notes

The Green at West Drayton is dominated by Britannia Court, the former Britannia Brewery which had its own 250 ft well. The frontage included one of the Green's 4 pubs. Number 15 nearby was West Drayton's first shop and only became a residence in 1972, having been run by the same family for nearly 200 years. St Catherine's church was built in 1869 for the many Irish Roman Catholics living around the Green.

Mill House, an impressive early 18th century building, stands on a narrow strip of land between Fray's river and the river Colne. The mill at the back was destroyed by fire in 1913 but the Colne can be seen (from a gate on the bridge) rushing beneath the wheels. Sir Allen Lane, founder of Penguin Books, had a flat in the house in the 1930s when he moved his fledgling company to Harmondsworth.

Harmondsworth means 'Heremod's Farm'. William the Conqueror gave the manor to Rouen Abbey, which established a small house south-west of the church. The church has a fine Norman doorway and tower base - its Tudor top has a Georgian cupola. The tithe barn (seen from the entrance to the manor house next door) is 191 ft long and dates from the 14th century. The Sun House, next to the church entrance, is Elizabethan and has served as a pub and a butcher's. The village still retains 2 pubs and a post office. The land to the south was still mainly market gardens when Sir Allen Lane moved his 2 year old Penguin Books from a London church crypt to a new site on the Bath Road. Building work was slow, as Sir Allen insisted on leaving the cabbages to mature since he had been forced to pay compensation for the crop. The present warehouse, extended in 1985, can hold over 40 million books. Now the village is probably best known for the Harmondsworth Detention Centre, where those arriving at Heathrow without valid entry papers are held. In the churchyard there is the tomb of Peggy Bedford (1782-1859) who ran *The King's Head* on the Bath Road. She once held the future Edward VII in her arms when Queen Victoria stopped there on her way to Windsor. Although her pub was burned down in 1934 her name lives on with *The Peggy Bedford* pub nearby. Also in the churchyard is the grave of Richard Cox, who developed the Cox's Orange Pippin apple at nearby Colnebrook in the 1830s.

West Drayton church, dedicated to St Martin, is mainly 15th century, with traces of the 13th century building which succeeded a Saxon church. In 1975 the interior was turned round and a freestanding altar placed at the west end - hence the new door. The Tudor gateway, twice used as the vicarage, was the entrance to the manor house built for Henry VIII's Secretary of State, Sir William Paget. Queen Elizabeth rode through the gateway in 1602.

Drayton Hall (recently 're-named' by developers refurbishing the house as offices) was rebuilt early in the 19th century to replace a 17th century house. The present house was the home of the lords of the manor, the De Burgh family, who entertained Napolean III here. Later the mansion was a school and an hotel before becoming the offices of the Yiewsley and West Drayton UDC. West Drayton became part of the London Borough of Hillingdon in 1965.

The Grand Union Canal

Introduction: Northolt has a remarkable rural centre, unseen from Western Avenue, and this fascinating walk along the historic Grand Union Canal is an excellent way of penetrating behind the urban facade of this part of Middlesex. Beginning on the Paddington arm of the canal, the route follows a rural corridor through Southall, Hayes, West Drayton, Cowley and Uxbridge.

When the canal was built at the beginning of the 19th century it completed a waterway between Birmingham and London, which for over a century carried freight traffic through the then rural countryside. Boatyards, wharves and factories sprang up along its length and in Middlesex, where the canal cut through the extensive clay deposits of the Thames valley, brickfields were an important local industry. Today the canal, now a vital environmental asset, carries only pleasure craft, but this walk provides intriguing reminders of our industrial heritage.

Distance: 10 miles which will take about 4 hours. There are, of course, no hills. However this is not a circular walk - the route ends at Uxbridge Underground station (Metropolitan and Piccadilly lines).

The route can easily be broken into 2 or more walks by using Hayes & Harlington and West Drayton BR stations on the parallel Paddington-Reading railway line.

Refreshments: There are pubs by many of the canal bridges. In Northolt the route passes the *Clock Café* and at Hayes there is a café just beyond the pub, north of the bridge. *Martha's Coffee Shop* is on the route in Uxbridge's Windsor Street. All 3 are open Mondays to Saturdays.

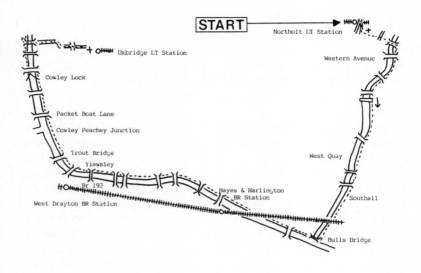

How to get there: The walk starts at Northolt Underground station (Central line) which is just north of Western Avenue (A10). There are no parking restrictions in the residential streets opposite the station.

The Walk: On leaving Northolt station turn right and, after a short distance, cross the main road using the crossing before bearing half-left down Ealing Road by the George VI Coronation clock. There is a small parade of shops, including a café, before the road runs down by a stream to *The Crown*. Turn left over the stream up to Northolt church.

Walk through the churchyard to enter Belvue Park opposite the church porch. Once on the green, which affords a view over Western Avenue to Greenford, turn left on a faint path which runs downhill. At a road go directly over to an enclosed path, which soon reaches the Paddington canal. Cross the bridge and turn right to join the towpath.

The water is to the right of the path as it runs south to go under Western Avenue. Almost at once the way is rural, with the houses of Greenford remaining some distance from the canal. After 4 bends the canal runs under the concrete Kensington Road bridge - a favourite perch for pigeons. Immediately after the Ruislip Road bridge, the canal is straddled by Taylor Woodrow's offices. Keep ahead and just at the beginning of King George's Fields on the left, two Canalway markers indicate the borough boundary. The towpath is now the boundary between Hillingdon on the right and Ealing. On the far side of the water, each side of the bend, there were canal arms serving brickfields.

Beyond a footbridge into the park is a view of West Quay Village, a marina development completed in 1989. Just before an iron bridge at the end of a park on the left, there are boundary markers showing where the borough boundary crosses the water. The path continues (soon with a better surface) towards a bridge beyond a TA centre. Southall's Broadway and High Street are to the left. Go under the bridge - once known as Hayes Bridge - to reach *The Hambrough Arms* and continue the walk. There is a new B&Q across the water on the site of Hayes Bridge Farm. At the end of the Bankside houses on the left the firm path is resumed and the canal bends south-west towards the Great Western Railway line. Just beyond the bridge there is a trace of one of the dock entrances which have now been filled in. Ahead is Bull's Bridge Junction.

Cross the bridge to pass a signpost pointing to Paddington, Brentford and Birmingham. Continue in the direction of Birmingham under the new Hayes bypass before passing high over the Yeading brook - the Ealing-Hillingdon boundary. Soon there is the Nestlé factory (and sometimes the smell of chocolate), where cocoa beans were once brought up by barge from Brentford Docks. After the main line railway bridge, the path rises to go over Chair Dock. Stay on the lower path to reach the bridge at Hayes - access to the hidden shops is up the steps just before the bridge. (At the top is *The Old Crown*. Hayes station is to the left over the bridge and there is a café to the right beyond the pub.)

The walk continues under the bridge where trees mask the buildings. Just before Printing House Lane Bridge there is a view of *The Blue Anchor*. At Dawley Road Bridge, *The Woolpack* has an appropriate sign. Beyond the whitewashed Rigby Lane Bridge, the canal is straight as it passes a helipad marked by red lights along the far fence. Round the bend is a new high concrete bridge which has obliterated Broad's Dock on the far side, which served a brickfield. Immediately beyond is Starveall's Bridge, with *The Foresters' Arms* at the top of the slope.

Here the parallel railway can often be heard from across the water. After Bridge 193, West Drayton station comes into view as the canal runs between West Drayton and Yiewsley on the towpath side. (Cross the next bridge for West Drayton station).

Just before West Drayton Bridge, the canal begins to turn north. At Trout Bridge, where a notice points to *The Jolly Anglers*, the path beneath is paved with tiles marked '1910'. After ¼ mile the canal crosses the line of the old West Drayton-Uxbridge railway branch just before reaching the Cowley Peachey Junction. There is a view down the straight Slough branch of the canal.

From now on there are numerous moorings and houseboats. Just before Packet Boat Lane at Cowley, the path rises over Packet Boat Dock opposite a boatyard and wine bar. *The Paddington Packet Boat* pub is to the right along the lane. Stay on the towpath which later passes under whitewashed Bridge 189 before reaching the first and only lock on the walk. Cowley Lock is the first on the climb up the Colne valley and just beyond the gates one can hear Fray's river crossing beneath. *The Shovel* has recently become part of The Harvester pub-restaurant chain. The path now crosses the bridge to continue on the west side of the canal, which is raised in order to be above the level of Fray's river. Beyond Mill Road Bridge (advertising *The Lord Hill*) the canal runs into Uxbridge. The approach to the main bridge is between *The General Eliott* on the towpath and a boatyard. Go under the bridge and turn left up a lane to the main road.

Cross the canal and pass *The Dolphin*. At the Fray's river bridge, cross over to the right side of the road ready to bear right at a huge road junction. Go over the footbridge and at the end of the far side ramp walk up Windsor Street. Uxbridge Underground station is beyond the church and Market House.

Historical Notes

The Canals: The Grand Junction Canal between Brentford on the Thames and Uxbridge opened in 1794. Through traffic to the Midlands was possible from 1800 and so successful was this venture that the 13 mile Paddington arm, ready for use the following year, was extended as the Regent's Canal in 1820. The companies amalgamated to form the Grand Union Canal Company in 1929 and since 1962 the British Waterways Board has been the canal authority.

Northolt was 'Northall', as opposed to 'Southall', up to the Tudor period. *The Load of Hay* pub on the workhouse site is a reminder that this area supplied hay to London early in the 19th century. With the cutting of the canal in 1801 transport was easy and this encouraged brickworks which lasted until 1939. The church, dating from the 13th century, stands in a delightful setting above the village green. The RAF airfield, for which the area is best known, opened in 1915. The Underground station opened in 1948 on the site of a GWR halt.

Southall's oldest building is the Elizabethan manor house now occupied by Southall Chamber of Commerce. The present church dates only from the turn of the 20th century. The canal on 2 sides of the town encouraged industrialisation, which in the 1950s and 1960s attracted Asian immigrants. The Martinware Pottery was on the Brentford canal bank from 1877 until 1923. The Wednesday cattle market, started in 1898, is famous for its horse sales.

Bull's Bridge was built in 1801 over the entrance to the Paddington canal. The 19th century cottage is a chandlery. The new industrial warehouses on the Paddington towpath side have replaced Tickner's Dock, belonging to a jam factory, and Kearley & Tonge's Mitre Dock, which were known as 'Jam Hole'.

Hayes lies to the north of the canal. St Martin's church has a 13th century chancel and wall paintings. Elizabeth I stayed at the 11th century manor house which partly survives in Church Street. The Great Western Railway line was built in 1838 but the station was not opened until 1864. Nestlés Avenue off Station Road is an example of the effect of massive industrialisation on the area.

West Drayton: See page 56.

Yiewsley: The *De Burgh Arms* and Yiewsley Grange are both 17th century. The church dates from 1858 when the area was still part of the Hillingdon parish. Following the arrival of the canal, the main industry was brickmaking and there were brick kilns on the main road between Thornton and Fairfield Roads.

Cowley Peachey Junction: The Slough Canal was built in 1882 as a straight 5 mile arm, free of locks.

Cowley lies between the river Colne to the west and the river Pinn to the east, with Fray's river and the canal also flowing through the village. Near the Pinn is the small 12th century church with a 1780 bellcote. A plaque on the outside west wall recalls William Dodd, George III's chaplain, who was hanged at Tyburn for forgery and buried here by his brother, who was the rector. *The Paddington Packet Boat* pub recalls the barge pulled by 4 horses which, at the beginning of the 19th century, ran daily to London from Packet Boat Dock and took precedence over all other traffic.

Uxbridge was an important stop on the London-Oxford road, with about 40 coaches a day calling in the 19th century. The 18th century Market House opposite the station is a reminder that this was the corn market town for many Middlesex and Buckinghamshire farmers. The church dates from the 14th century and has a recent addition of an arts centre called The Nave. *The Crown & Treaty House* pub was the scene of an abortive peace negotiation between Royalists and Roundheads in 1645. The long established Thomas Barnard secondhand bookshop in Windsor Street is housed in a 300 year old building.

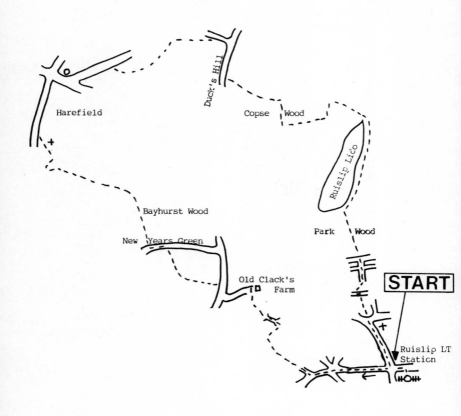

Harefield

Duck's Hill

Copse   Wood

Ruislip Lido

Bayhurst Wood

Park   Wood

New Years Green

Old Clack's
Farm

START

Ruislip LT
Station

Ruislip

Introduction: North-west Middlesex is still agricultural land, its open, hilly countryside providing an invigorating walk which begins at the attractive commuter town of Ruislip. The walk soon leaves the town behind, striking out across fields and through woodland, over the river Pinn. The way may be muddy in places and you should be prepared for a missing footbridge. There are rewarding views to be discovered, including eastwards to Harrow on the Hill. The route also takes in the attractive village of Harefield, still isolated on the ridge overlooking the Colne valley and with picturesque almshouses and 13th century church. Returning to Ruislip, the tree-fringed waters of the Lido can be seen.

Distance: 8½ miles, a circular walk which will take about 4 hours. There are several steep hills.

Refreshments: There are several pubs and a fish and chip shop in Harefield. The *Village Tea Rooms* is opposite Ruislip church and there is a café next to Ruislip's Great Barn - both are passed towards the end of the route.

How to get there: Ruislip is on the A4180. The walk begins at Ruislip Underground station (Metropolitan and Piccadilly lines) where there is a car park.

The Walk: At the end of Ruislip station's approach road go left to the crossroads at the bottom of the High Street (right). Go ahead up a residential road known as Kingsend. Continue forward at a

5-way road junction, by *The White Bear* (on the left) and *The Orchard*, into Ickenham Road. At a garage on the left, turn right up an unmarked lane (known as Hill Lane and used as an entrance to Ruislip Golf Centre).

Walk past Harwell Close on the right and the Golf Centre on the left to continue forward on the rough lane. At a junction do not go right with the lane but keep ahead on a narrow footpath running up a wide enclosed way (known as Clack Lane). Beyond lonely footpath signs the way reaches a crosspath. Keep forward on the path which bears half-right to meet the river Pinn.

Cross the footbridge and bear half-right across the meadow to a stile near a house. (Ignore the path running up the field.) Climb over the stile, opposite a private garden gateway, and go right up the narrow path. The way opens out to meet the end of a lane at Old Clacks Farm. Turn left up the lane (known as Tile Kiln Lane). Soon the road becomes metalled at a junction and after a sharp right turn meets a main road.

Turn right for a few yards to go over a stile on the left. This path, which runs up to Pylon Farm at the top of the hill, is extremely boggy and the farmyard notoriously muddy. Walkers may wish to continue along the main road and turn left into New Years Green Lane.

Those staying on the footpath should head for the signpost seen against the sky to the left of the farmhouse buildings. Walk towards the start of the hedge boundary, which should be on the left. On approaching, beware of very boggy ground - sometimes there is a plank to help walkers. On the way up the hill there is an iron gate to pass through or climb over. At the top of the hill there is a view eastwards to Harrow on the Hill. Go over the 2 stiles by the signpost and ahead past the cowshed on the right, and turn right along its side. Before reaching the bungalow, bear left for a few yards and over a stile. Go half-left over a field to a stile in the corner by New Years Green Lane.

Turn left along the lane past 2 houses and at a bend turn right to the start of a dual path - a parallel footpath and bridleway. Go over the stile and keep close to the fence on the right. There are a couple of stiles at streams before the path runs close to Bayhurst Wood. Beyond the surprise view of picnic tables in the wood, go over the stile into the wood and turn left to pass a pond.

Keep forward beyond the pond on the left, on a path which at first runs parallel to a horse track. Stay by the fence on the left as much as possible. After nearly ¼ mile turn left out of the wood and up a stepped path to a stile. Follow the low fence on the right over open ground. To the right there is a view of the partly 16th century Breakspear House.

Go over the stile and past an overgrown stile on a steep slope. The path runs ahead uphill to another stile and on to a viewpoint above Park Lodge Farm. Go over 2 stiles and down the next field. Stay by the hedge and ignore the stile on the left. A stile by a gate leads into a second field and at the next corner go over the stile by the gate on the left. Walk along the side of a field to a redundant stile and bear half-right to a stile under a tree. Turn right along the gravel track and at a junction turn left to pass the entrance to the Australian war cemetery and Harefield church.

Continue up the road and bear right up the hill into the village. The pavement runs behind the almshouses. At the green, turn right into Breakspear Road to pass *The Swan* and the village pond. Go right into Northwood Road and walk as far as the last house on the right. Go through the gate just beyond this house and before the entrance to Shepherds Hill House.

A path runs along a fence and past several gardens to a stile. Turn left to follow a hedge at the side of a field. At an unexpected narrow field corner go over a stile and turn right to follow a hedge (to the right) in another field. The path, with a good view, runs gently downhill past a wood and under overhanging trees. At the bottom go over a stream (where the footbridge may still be broken) and a fixed iron gate. Continue up the next field by a hedge on the left. At the top go over the stile in the narrow corner and turn right downhill by a hedge (keeping it on your right). There is another stile on the way, before reaching a stile at the bottom leading on to an overgrown lane. (There may be some rubble piled here.)

Do not follow the lane but bear slightly right to a stile by a gate. The way is across a paddock and over another stile before climbing the hill. At the top the field narrows to a couple of stiles and rejoins the lane. Turn right up the lane, which soon opens out into the residential Jackets Lane. At a main road - Duck's Hill - go right to the last house on the left.

Follow the signposted bridleway which runs along a line of back gardens on the edge of Copse Wood. Ignore the early signposts, and after just over ¼ mile the path turns left with the gardens and joins a more substantial path. After a few yards go right to leave the houses and follow a wide path into the wood. After nearly ¼ mile the path climbs and narrows by a slight clearing. Do not go ahead on the narrow path but turn left on to another path, which soon runs downhill and opens out. This straight path runs to the eastern side of the wood.

On emerging into the open, turn left up a very wide way to reach a pond just beyond a signpost. Go right over a footbridge, but before the golf course turn right on to an easily missed path in the trees. A winding path runs over a concrete bridge to a 3-way signpost. Turn right to go along the side of a low building (a firing range, keep it on your left).

The path runs through woodland and soon turns on to the edge of the golf course. Follow the high wire fence of the nature reserve on your right. Turn right over a stream with the fence. After a short distance the path leaves the grass of the golf course to become more defined in the trees. Beyond a junction, the path continues by the fence (still on the right), through which can be seen the recently laid narrow gauge railway line. Later there is a view through the fence and trees to Ruislip Lido.

On reaching Woody Bay station turn left away from the railway on to a path running up through the trees. Stay on the main path and ignore any turnings - especially to the left. After just over ¼ mile the way passes close to houses on the right, before running up a short concrete path to a residential road.

Go directly ahead down Sherwood Avenue. At the far end do not go left on the signposted path but half-right, through the trees to a road by the river Pinn. Cross the road to a footpath sign and bear half-left across the grass to briefly join a concrete access road. Go up the metalled path on the left at the side of the Winston Churchill Hall, to join the farmhouse driveway which passes the 2 barns. Ahead is the High Street, leading to the crossroads by Ruislip station.

Historical Notes

Ruislip: As a result of the railway arriving in 1904 there is much suburban housing, but the old village can still be found in the middle. The moated farmhouse and 13th century Great Barn - the oldest in Middlesex - belonged to Bec Abbey in France from the Conquest to the Reformation. The church was built about 1250 but its font is a hundred years older. In the north aisle is a 1697 bread cupboard for the poor which remained in use until 1955. *The Swan* is 16th century, along with several other buildings in the High Street - best seen from inside the churchyard.

Harefield: The east end of the church dates from the 13th century and inside there are box pews and a Georgian pulpit. On the right of the high altar is the tomb of the Countess of Derby, who in 1600 built the almshouses on Church Hill. There are 17th century cottages in the High Street and the timber-framed *King's Arms* on the green dates from the same period. The hospital stands on the site of a temporary First World War hospital for Australians, and 111 are buried in the churchyard, where Anzac Day is observed annually.

Ruislip Lido: The boating lake was dug in 1811 as a feeder for the Grand Junction Canal nearby.

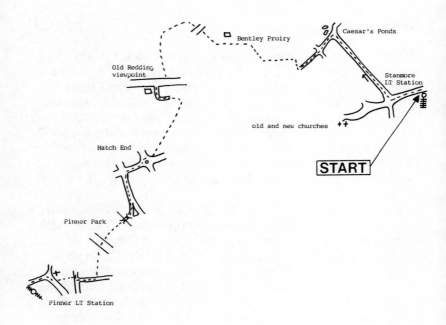

Caesar's Ponds

Bentley Proiry

Stanmore
LT Station

Old Redding
viewpoint

old and new churches

START

Hatch End

Pinner Park

Pinner LT Station

Bentley Priory

Introduction: Harrow Weald once stretched across the north of Middlesex, densely wooded hunting country for kings and noblemen. This exhilarating walk from Stanmore to Pinner offers wonderful views over the surrounding countryside, and you may also be fortunate enough to encounter deer along the route. From Stanmore the walk follows a woodland path upwards towards Bentley Priory, founded in the 12th century and the RAF base during the Second World War from which the Battle of Britain was controlled. From here, on a clear day, the City of London is visible, 11 miles to the south-west. At Harrow Weald Common you can look down upon the Middlesex-Hertfordshire boundary in the valley below. Old Redding is the next viewpoint to be reached, with extensive views over Hertfordshire, Harrow and Horsenden Hill. The route continues through Hatch End village, with 17th century Letchford House, and Pinner Park, before descending into the attractive town of Pinner.

Distance: 5 miles which will take about 3 hours if the opportunity is taken to pause at the viewpoints. There is a hill near the start at Stanmore. However this is not a circular walk - the route ends at Pinner Underground station (Metropolitan line).

Refreshments: *Canelle* tearoom is open daily in Church Road in Great Stanmore. At the natural half-way point, the Old Redding viewpoint, there is *The Case is Altered* pub. *Brooks* teashop (closed Sundays) can be found in the passageway to Sainsbury's off Pinner High Street.

How to get there: The walk starts at Stanmore Underground station (Jubilee line). Stanmore is on the A10 west of the A5. Limited parking is available off the main road in Stanmore.

The Walk: On leaving Stanmore station turn left along the main road to the traffic lights at the beginning of The Broadway. Turn right up Dennis Lane, which soon runs uphill between residential Stanmore on the left and the countryside.

The lane leads up to a junction by Caesar's Ponds at Little Common. Bear left with Wood Lane and over to the right can be seen a cluster of houses including 18th and 19th century cottages. Soon the pavement passes entrances on the left to Stanmore Hall.

At the main road - the top of Stanmore Hill - cross straight over into Aylmer Drive. The road runs downhill (passing Adelaide Close, named after the Queen who lived at Bentley Priory) to a kissing gate. At the bottom of the ramp turn left (with your back to the road) to walk through the trees for a few yards and find a crosspath. At once turn right to pass a waymark post and after a short distance the woodland path bears left just before a deer park fence.

The path leaves the trees to enjoy a grass surface as it runs downhill with the deer park on the right. The way becomes stepped as it rises to a junction. Turn right on to a metalled path to stay with the deer fence and climb gently uphill for just over ¼ mile.

At a junction, by the Bentley Priory Circular Walk information board, turn left on to an unfenced narrow concrete footpath which runs along by the Bentley Priory grounds. After a short distance there is an excellent view of the mansion. Soon the way curves steeply downhill, before climbing more gently to give a view on clear days of the City of London, 11 miles away to the south-west.

Beyond a kissing gate the path turns north along a wooded path. At the far end, go through the wooden gate and cross the main road with care to the gap almost opposite. Go down the steps from the road and still keep in a northerly direction through the trees. The path is not always clear. Stay to the left of a bench but do not be tempted to bear left. Instead keep forward to find a lonely waymark post in the trees. Still keep ahead to a second waymark at the junction with a more substantial path. Turn left to follow this path near the northern boundary of the wood, known as Harrow Weald Common. Soon the way is hard up against the boundary hedge, giving a view of the Middlesex-Hertfordshire boundary in the green valley.

Just beyond 2 houses, the way bears left to a junction. To the right is a former entrance to Grim's Dyke and to the left is a path marked by 2 white posts. Take the long straight path ahead. The way rises gently to a road known as Old Redding. Turn right to *The Case Is Altered*. On the far side of the pub (on your left) there is a viewpoint and picnic tables.

The walk continues down a wide signposted lane at the side of *The Case Is Altered*. The way bears left at Copse Farm. Do not be tempted by the signpost to 'Suzanne's car park' but keep ahead for a few more yards to where the lane bends sharply. Go ahead here through a white kissing gate where a signpost points to 'Oxhey Lane'.

Keep forward for a short distance and bear right by a building down to a stile beyond an oak tree. Climb over the stile and keep to the hedge on the left. After a second stile the path becomes enclosed as it runs under a long line of oaks. At the far end go over a stile to a major road junction.

Turn right to cross the end of Oxhey Lane and at once bear left to cross Uxbridge Road. Now walk in a westerly direction (right) along the main road, using the parallel Boniface Walk pavement. Just before the next junction there is St Teresa's church on the left and Hatch End Free church on the opposite side of the roundabout. Bear left on the Boniface Walk pavement to turn south into Headstone Lane.

Bear half-right by 17th century Letchford House to walk up Letchford Terrace and pass *The Letchford Arms* on the right. At the end go right to cross the high footbridge over the Euston main line.

On the far side a narrow footpath runs ahead to a metalled lane. Keep forward through 2 side gates to continue ahead on a wide farm path which runs through Pinner Park Farm. Here the way is often muddy. Beyond the milk float garage and milking parlour on the right, the path enjoys a clean metalled surface. At the farm entrance go straight across the dual carriageway and over the stile opposite. A straight (and often muddy path) leads ahead to a second stile before climbing with a grass surface up to a viewpoint behind Pinner. Beyond the gates at the top are 2 seats from which to enjoy the view back to Old Redding.

To continue, bear right into a road - Wakeham's Hill - which soon runs down to a T-junction with Moss Lane. Cross over and go right for a few yards to find the entrance to a footpath. Follow this narrow enclosed path to Church Lane and turn right. Just beyond Pinner House (on the right) is Pinner church. Bear left into the High Street and at the bottom of the hill go left for Pinner Underground station.

Historical Notes

Great Stanmore lies just west of Watling Street and here on high ground Julius Caesar is believed to have won a battle against the Celts. 'Stanmore' means 'stoney mere' and the ponds (or meres) at the top of Stanmore Hill are known as Caesar's Ponds. A mound in nearby Lime House, once home of aircraft pioneer Handley Page, is referred to as 'Boadicea's Tomb'. Broadway Cottages, in The Broadway near Marsh Lane, are Tudor. In the grounds of the early Victorian St John's church is the abandoned brick church paid for by Sir John Wolstenholme of Wolstenholme Cape fame and consecrated by Archbishop Laud in 1632. Sir Nikolaus Pevsner considered it to be one of the best ruins in Middlesex. WS Gilbert of Gilbert & Sullivan is buried outside the new church's south door.

Stanmore Hall is the successor to a house built by Handel's patron, the Duke of Chandos, for his wife's widowhood. The present castle-style house dates from 1843, with major additions in 1890 for William Knox D'Arcy, founder of BP. William Morris and

Edward Burne Jones were involved with the interior decoration. The building has recently been restored as offices after a serious fire in 1979.

Bentley Priory, now part of RAF Stanmore, was founded about 1170 as a branch of the monastery at Canterbury Cathedral. The monastic community was further down the hill to the south and the main building was only moved to its present site under secular ownership in 1775. Soon afterwards Sir John Soane remodelled the house for the 1st Lord Abercorn, whose many guests included the Duke of Wellington, Sarah Siddons and Lady Hamilton. This was the last home of William IV's widow, Queen Adelaide, who died here in 1849. Her visitors included the young Queen Victoria and Prince Albert. In 1882, after the addition of the tower, the mansion became an hotel. The Air Ministry purchased the property in 1925 and it was from here, high above London, that Lord Dowding controlled the Battle of Britain in 1940.

Old Redding is on the edge of wooded Harrow Weald Common - 'weald' means 'wood'. On the north side of the road is 'The City', a 5-sided area which was a brick and tile works in the 17th and 18th centuries. The name was probably a reflection on the self-contained business, with workers living on-site. The pub was sometimes referred to as the 'Cathedral'. Its real name is *The Case is Altered* - a corruption of 'Casa Alta' meaning appropriately 'high house'. Although there is a panoramic view from the pub's back window there is an even more extensive one from the public viewpoint just to the west of the pub. Harrow on the Hill is to the south-west. Immediately behind the viewpoint is the entrance to the Norman Shaw-designed Grims Dyke House, built for the painter Frederick Goodall and later home of WS Gilbert, who died whilst rescuing a guest from the lake.

Hatch End means 'area by a gate' - maybe Pinner Park's gate. The oldest building is Letchford House, built in 1670 as Hatch End Farmhouse, which was restored as offices in 1975.

75

Pinner Park was probably enclosed for deer by William the Conqueror. During Elizabeth I's reign the park was in the possession of Sir Nicholas Bacon and his son Francis, the Lord Chancellor. The estate remains green as the home of Hall & Sons Dairy.

Pinner is famous for its annual fair dating back to 1336 and held in the High Street on the Wednesday of Spring Bank Holiday week. *The Queen's Head* is Tudor, but the date - 1705 - on the splendid sign refers to the year when Queen Anne changed horses there. The largely 14th century parish church remains a daughter church of nearby Harrow. The prominent and much noted 'coffin in the air' built outside in 1809 is in fact only a decorative feature above a conventional burial. East End Farm Cottage in Moss Lane is the oldest timber-framed cottage in Middlesex. There is a blue plaque on 75 Moss Lane where 'inventor' and comic artist Heath Robinson lived from 1913-1918.

Potters Bar

Introduction: Potters Bar and the village of South Mimms are in the most northerly corner of Middlesex and this country walk traces the old county boundary with Hertfordshire. Potters Bar was just a hamlet on the Great North Road until the railway came in the mid 19th century, and open countryside is still easily reached from the town. Stout shoes are recommended as the footpath at one point fords the Mimmshall brook. At times following the course of the brook, and passing close by the site of a Norman castle, the route crosses open fields to South Mimms, with its 12th century church and almshouses. The path then continues through woodland, with open views towards Hatfield from Hawkshead Wood, rejoining the Mimmshall brook and making its way gradually downhill back to Potters Bar.

Distance: 6 miles, a circular walk which will take about 3 hours. The hills are gentle climbs.

Refreshments: There is *The Potters* pub opposite the station in Potters Bar. South Mimms has 2 pubs.

How to get there: Potters Bar is off Junction 24 on the M25. Parking is possible on the main road west of the station and in side roads. The walk starts at Potters Bar BR station on the King's Cross line.

The Walk: Walk up the west side of the station through the car park. Soon there is a clearly marked path by the fence on the right. Beyond the extensive car park the way becomes enclosed.

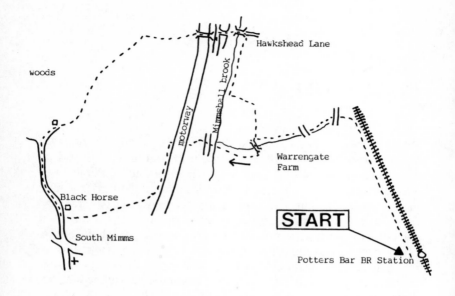

Do not be tempted off the path at the first sight of countryside but continue on past houses and a small industrial estate. On joining a road, at the bottom of a slope, at once cross over and go through a gap immediately to the left of the high WH Smith News gateway. Pass over a stream and turn left to walk between the stream and the high fence on the right. The narrow path leads to a road. Climb over the stile opposite and at once go right to continue with the stream on the left. The uneven path leads to a field and Warrengate Farm comes into view beyond the stream.

On reaching a bridge at the farm, cross the stream to follow the opposite bank ahead. Beyond a barn on the left, the way bears right with the stream and after ¼ mile reaches Mimmshall brook at a ford. Walk through the water and go ahead to the iron gates. Climb over the stile at the side and cross the road to go through (or over if locked) iron gates almost opposite. A concrete road runs downhill to pass under the motorway. At the end of the tunnel bear left up a slope to follow the motorway fence on the left. (The

78

right turning from the tunnel leads to the site of a Norman castle.) Where the concrete road swings away, still keep ahead.

Beyond a wooden gateway bear right with a rough track which runs over open land before becoming more defined. Eventually the path passes close to a hedge on the left and over a stile by a gate. Keep forward to a hidden wooden stile to the left of the tree in front of the line of houses. Climb over the stile and walk down a short residential drive to Blackhorse Lane in South Mimms.

The church and village centre is out of view to the left. The walk continues to the right past *The Black Horse*. Beyond the houses the lane narrows and climbs up to a junction by a grass triangle. Bear right towards a gateway and a lodge, but just before the gateway turn off to the right on a narrow footpath.

The way soon widens as it runs past farm buildings on the right and climbs just inside a wood. From this point the path marks the boundary between Middlesex and Hertfordshire and the division between the newer Mymmshall Wood on the right and Hawkshead Wood, which is in places darkened even on a sunny day by the firs. Ignore a turning to the left and after just over ½ mile Hawkshead Wood falls away to give a fine view towards Hatfield. The path narrows and runs downhill to a field. Turn right to follow a curving field boundary down to the bridleway bridge over the motorway.

On the far side turn left up the road and then right down a narrow lane (with a wide entrance). This short lane lies just outside Middlesex - at the bottom of the hill there is a City Post on the right confirming the old county boundary. Go ahead over the bridge at the start of Hawkshead Lane. On the far side go over a stile on the right and follow the Mimmshall brook (on the right).

Continue into the second field and at the far end turn left up the field boundary to the lonely group of trees at the top of the hill. Just beyond the trees, bear right on to a more substantial path, which soon runs downhill to Warrengate Farm. Turn left just before the bridge to follow the outward route back into Potters Bar.

Historical Notes

Potters Bar Was 'Potterbare' in 1386 but the earliest pottery here is not recorded until 1658, at the south end of the High Street. This was a hamlet on the Great North Road until the railway arrived in 1850, with a station built at the last minute as an afterthought and considered to be outside the village until new building in the 1930s. Ruined St John's church in the old centre was built in 1835 and is now the war memorial. On the corner of Mutton Lane and Dugdale Hill Lane there is the church of King Charles the Martyr - one of only 7 such dedications - built in 1939 in the style of a Jacobean barn.

South Mimms: The remains of Norman Geoffrey de Mandeville's castle is by the motorway to the north-west of the village. In the Domesday Book, 'Mimms' is spelt 'Mimes' and today there is the nearby North Mymms. The church, restored by GE Street, dates from 1136 and is noted for its pre-Reformation Frowyk tombs. The chest in the nave may be as old as the church and therefore the oldest piece of furniture in Middlesex. Next door are the Brewers' Almshouses which were moved here from Kitts End near Wrotham Park in 1856. The village, now bypassed by long distance traffic, was once on the main London-Barnet-St Albans-Holyhead coaching route.

Enfield Chase

Introduction: Enfield Chase, in the north-east of Middlesex, was an ancient hunting forest, much loved by Tudor kings and queens. Now the countryside survives as common, parkland and farmland. This walk begins at Trent Park, a landscaped estate with a marvellous 18th century mansion and grounds originally laid out by Humphry Repton. Woodland paths, streams, lakes and views across to Epping Forest enhance this part of the walk. Via Camlet Hill and Ash Wood, the route leads to West Lodge Park. The first house on this site was built in 1399, and was one of the four lodges which guarded entrances to the Chase. The 19th century arboretum contains over 2,000 trees and is open to the public twice a year. The walk continues to Hadley Wood, past the original Victorian houses, and on to Monken Hadley Common, the western edge of the Chase. It is particularly beautiful in autumn, when golden beech leaves carpet the ground.

Distance: 6½ miles, a circular walk which will take about 3 hours. There are 2 hills to climb.

Refreshments: Trent Park's café is open throughout the year and is best reached at the end of the walk. *The Cock* pub is also towards the end of the walk, but Hadley Wood has an excellent baker's, with drinks on sale at the nearby newsagent.

How to get there: Trent Park is on the A111 with parking just inside the main entrance. Those arriving by car should make their way to the nature trail to join the walk. The main walk starts at Oakwood Underground station (Piccadilly line).

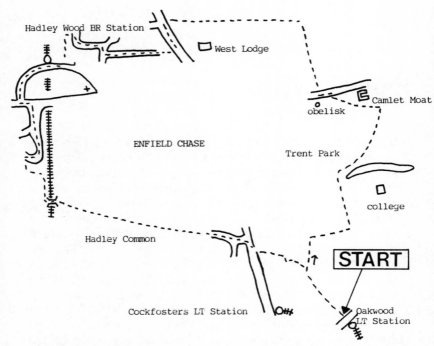

The Walk: Enter Trent Park by the entrance directly opposite Oakwood Underground station. A gravel footpath runs ahead across the grass and past a pond on the left to enter a pine wood. The path runs downhill to cross the first of several streams, before following the side of a field.

Keep left near the railway at open ground. The path crosses a stream and later enters a wood to cross 2 further streams. Here the railway swings away as the path continues ahead over open ground. After the next bridge bear half-right towards the far corner and Church Wood. To the right there is a view across Enfield to Epping Forest. A short narrow path leads to a substantial woodland walk. Turn right on this path, which runs down and then up hill.

Beyond a junction of paths, the way is a straight path through a belt of oak trees. Just beyond a gateway turn left on to grass.

To the left are tennis courts. Cross the main Trent Park driveway (by a shuttered lodge on the right) and take the path ahead signposted 'Nature Trail & Lakes'. The way runs downhill on the edge of a wood.

At the nature trail entrance (by an information board) a path to the left leads to the café, ½ mile away.

The walk continues ahead on the main path, which after a double bend runs in the open above a lake. As a path joins from the right there is a view north (left) up to the obelisk. Stay on the main path (do not bear right) to walk uphill through the edge of a wood on to Camlet Hill. Keep on through Moat Wood to a crosspath by an information board. There are toilets ahead.

Turn left on to a narrower path, which soon runs close to the remains of Camlet Moat on the right. On approaching a field do not bear left with the main path (except to reach the obelisk and see the view from its base) but turn right towards the road. Go through the kissing gate and turn left along the road to draw level with the obelisk. Cross over to the layby to find a stile.

Climb over the stile to follow the enclosed path which runs downhill passing, on the way, the edge of Ash Wood. At the bottom of the hill turn left on to another enclosed path which follows the field boundary. Ahead is a view of West Lodge. Apart from a break for a farm track, the fenced way runs ahead for ¾ mile to the main road beyond West Lodge Park. Opposite this final stile is Waggons Road.

Turn left along the main road past a bus stop and, before the West Lodge Park entrance, cross the road to look for a footpath between numbers 439 and 441. The path soon crosses the Monken Mead brook to join a cul-de-sac in Hadley Wood. Follow this residential road - a reminder of what could have befallen the rest of the Chase - to the far end at Duchy Road. Turn right over the brook and at once go left into Courtleigh Avenue. Just beyond Hadley Wood school, turn left up a footpath leading to a green open space. Turn left to follow the path downhill to a road in the centre of Hadley Wood, where the original Victorian houses are to be found.

Turn right to pass the station and village shops and continue round the crescent to the main through road. Go left for a few yards before turning right down Parkgate Avenue. Continue past the Parkgate Crescent turning on the right and just after the road bears right look for a path between numbers 61 and 59 on the left. Walk up the alleyway into the woods of Monken Hadley Common.

Keep forward on the woodland path, but after crossing a stream bear left towards the railway. At the fence follow the railway on the left for 200 yards to a bridge.

Turn left past the gate and over the railway bridge. The path runs gently downhill through a wooded hollow - carpeted with golden beech leaves in the autumn. After almost ½ mile the way crosses a narrow bridge below Beech Hill Lake (on the left above the bank). Continue ahead up the hill (where the way may not be immediately clear due to fallen trees). The path soon becomes a metalled road before reaching Hadley Common's eastern gateway. Follow the road to a junction by *The Cock* (on the right) and turn left into Chalk Lane to reach the main road. Turn right along Cockfosters Road to Trent Park's main entrance. Cockfosters Underground station is ¼ mile ahead.

To reach the Trent Park café follow the drive and keep left at the fork.

Those wishing to return to Oakwood station should go through the Trent Park gateway and at once bear half-right across the grass. In the far corner take a waymarked path running into the trees which bends to the left. After a short distance turn right on to a path, which soon runs out of the trees and across a field to join the outward route.

Historical Notes

Enfield Chase is bounded by Monken Hadley in the west, Enfield in the east, Coopers Lane Road in the north and Oakwood in the south. At the time of the Conquest, 4,000 pigs were run here, feeding on acorns and crab apples. Geoffrey de Mandeville of South Mimms turned the woodland into a chase shortly afterwards. It was enclosed as a deer park about 1140 and in 1399 became part of the Duchy of Lancaster through Henry IV's marriage to Mary of Bohun. Henry VIII and his daughter Princess Elizabeth hunted here. The future Elizabeth I once rode over from Hatfield in a 152-strong party comprising 12 ladies in white satin, 120 liveried yeomen and 20 archers. Large scale poaching in the 18th century resulted in the Chase being divided up for farming in 1777.

Trent Park: George III, as Duke of Lancaster, granted this part of Enfield Chase to his doctor, Sir Richard Webb. He had attended the Duke of Gloucester at Trento in Italy and so called his new home Trent Park. The house was designed by William Chambers and the grounds by Humphry Repton. Much of the landscaping seen today dates from 1833, when the Quaker banker David Bevan purchased the property by accident when nodding at the wrong moment during an auction. This century more changes were made by Sir Philip Sassoon who brought the obelisks from Wrest Park in Bedfordshire and refaced the mansion with bricks from the demolished Devonshire House in Piccadilly. During the Second World War, Rudolf Hess was interrogated at the house, which is now part of Middlesex Polytechnic. The estate, which includes Camlet Moat, site of a hunting lodge featured in Sir Walter Scott's *Fortunes of Nigel*, was saved after the Second World War by the Middlesex County Council.

West Lodge Park: The first house on this site was built in 1399 for Enfield Chase's West Bailey Ranger. Henry VIII often stayed here. In the 17th century it was the home of Charles II's Secretary of State, Henry Coventry, when diarist John Evelyn visited and recorded: 'It is a very pretty place...that which I most admired was that in all the Chase within 14 miles of London there is not a house, barn, church or building'. Through much of the 18th century it was owned by the Dukes of Chandos, who held the office of Chief Ranger. The 3rd Duke's widow continued to live here until 1808, long after the Chase had been divided up. The present building dates from 1838 and its arboretum, started in the 1880s, has 2,000 trees embracing 350 varieties. West Lodge is now an hotel and the arboretum is open twice a year on a Sunday in June and October as part of the National Gardens Scheme.

Hadley Wood: Soon after the Great Northern Railway was cut through here in 1850, farmer Charles Jack obtained a new lease from the Duchy of Lancaster to develop his land if a station was built. Hadley Wood station opened in 1884 with just 50 houses. Duchy Road and Lancaster Avenue recall the original landlord, and the Duchy still holds a few freeholds. Hadley Wood Golf Clubhouse was originally the residence of George III's Duchy Surveyor. A post office and village shop opened in 1892 and St Paul's church followed in 1911. The total number of houses is now just over 900.

Forty Hall

Introduction: Forty Hall, in the north-eastern corner of Middlesex, is said to be one of the best examples of 17th century domestic architecture in the country, built for St Nicholas Rainton, a Lord Mayor of London. This part of Middlesex is still noted for its horticulture, which has helped to preserve the tranquillity of the area.

This gentle walk explores the grounds of Forty Hall, enhanced by river, lakes and woodland. Eighteenth century Theobalds, with London's Temple Bar erected at its northern entrance, is close by. From the New river, an artificial watercourse cut in the 17th century to provide London with water, there are views across the Lee valley. The route also follows the Roman Ermine Street for a time, before passing 19th century Myddleton House on the way back to Turkey Street.

Distance: 7¼ miles, a circular walk which will take about 3½ hours. There are some gentle hills.

Refreshments: There is *The Crown & Tinker* in Whitewebbs Lane and *The Pied Bull* at Bulls Cross. There are 2 pubs, *The Plough* and *The Turkey*, at Turkey Street. The café at Forty Hall is open daily except Mondays.

How to get there: Turkey Street lies between the A10 and the A1010. The walk starts at Turkey Street BR station on the Liverpool Street line.

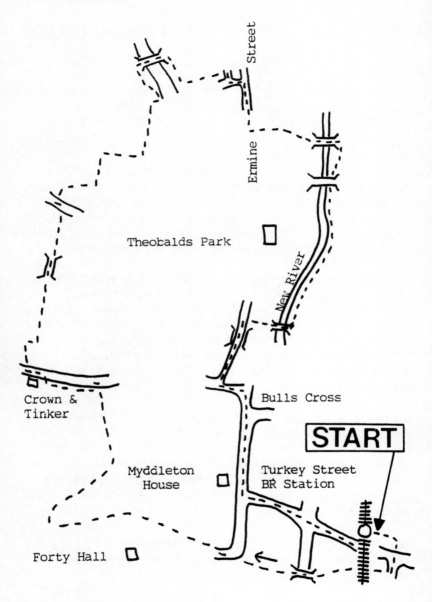

The Walk: From the turnstile exit at Turkey Street station, go ahead to a path at the side of the Turkey brook and cross the footbridge to reach the main street. Cross over into Winnington Road and after a short distance go right where a sign points to 'Grenville Cottages'.

Pass under the railway line and keep ahead past the Enfield Crematorium gates on the left to follow an enclosed metalled footpath. Later the fence ends to reveal the Turkey brook on the right. Cross the Great Cambridge Road on the footbridge and continue ahead on an unfenced footpath beyond a kissing gate. After crossing the New river (hidden in a pipeline) the path meets a road by Forty Hall parish hall.

Cross over by the traffic lights to find a path leading into the grounds of Forty Hall. Bear right to the Turkey brook before continuing eastwards along the river bank. Soon there is a first glimpse of the mansion to the left, in the trees. There is a final view of the house just as the path descends below a bank on the left to run between the river and the lakes.

The now woodland path continues by the brook for ¼ mile to a bridge. Go right over the Turkey brook and ahead on the path to the left of an iron gate. This path, known as the 'Mile And A Half Alley', runs north and then east before crossing the old course of the New river, which flowed through the garden of Myddleton House. The path then continues through trees and on to a stile at Whitewebbs Lane. Turn left along the road for a few yards to join a bridle path. Walk on a narrow metalled path parallel with both the bridleway and the road on the right. Soon after the narrow path joins the bridleway, bear right on to a pavement by the road.

At *The Crown & Tinker* cross the road to go over a stile by a stable yard. The narrow path runs ahead and beyond a couple of stiles passes a cottage on the left. On drawing level with a miniature windmill, the path makes a sharp right turn. Beyond a stile go left to follow a field boundary. At the corner do not go through the gate but over the stile. Keep by the left hand side of the field and walk down into the valley. Climb over the stile and pipes carrying a stream to walk ahead, past an oak tree and out of Middlesex into Hertfordshire.

A footbridge carries the path over the M25. From the gate and the top of the steps there is a view south to the City of London. Continue north up the side of the field. When the trees on the left end, the path bears slightly left towards Theobalds manor.

At the lane, known as Oldpark Ride, turn left for a few yards towards the Theobalds Estate notice before turning right through a wide gap. Bear over to the left, not to go through the gate but to follow the side of Home Wood. The path runs gently downhill with a good view. Where the trees end, turn left to follow the east side of the wood. At the far end of the field turn right and just before the next corner go left over a ditch into a sloping field.

Walk ahead under the line of oaks to the bottom of the field, where there is a hidden stile by a gate. Go over the stile and follow a track uphill towards Broadfield Farm. Go over another stile into the farmyard. Keep ahead past a building on the left and turn right towards the fence of the main road in a cutting. At once turn left to go over a stile and follow a narrow path by the road fence. The path joins the concrete farm drive. At a road (by glasshouses) turn right over the main road to the outskirts of Bury Green, a suburb of Cheshunt.

At once turn right along the side of a main road to draw level with the farm buildings across the cutting. Do not go through the gate ahead but turn left through a gap into a grassy open space. Keep ahead along the boundary (on the right) to an enclosed footpath at the next corner. After 250 yards the way meets a road on a housing estate. Go right and then left down to a T-junction, opposite a house called 'Noss Mayo'.

Turn right along this older residential road (which roughly follows the Roman Ermine Street). When the road becomes a rough lane, continue past the 'Private Road' sign and Bury Green Farmhouse on the left. Just before the bottom of the hill, near the fenced main road, go left on to a narrow path signposted 'Theobalds Lane'. The path runs along the side of a wood on the right, to a wooden stile. Bear half-right across a field to a kissing gate by the New river. Cross the water using the new bridge, where there

is a view north to the landmark towers of the church and former
Lady Huntingdon's Connection building at Cheshunt's Churchgate.

Turn south on the grass waterside path to walk downstream under
the main road and over Theobalds Lane. Being an artificial river,
the path is unusually high and affords a view across the Lee valley
to the left. After just over ¼ mile there is a brief view on the right
of the Theobalds Park mansion. Over to the left of the river can
be seen a fenced but overgrown footpath running towards the
footbridge ahead.

Go over this, the first footbridge, and follow an enclosed path
running alongside the wood. At the end cross a lonely cut-off
section of Ermine Street and go up the steps to a road. Turn left
to cross the M25 and re-enter Middlesex. On the far side can be
seen a Theobalds Park lodge by the former drive, which followed
the Roman road. At the junction with Whitewebbs Lane cross over
and turn left.

The path is briefly separated from the road by a hedge before
the lane swings right on to the Roman road at Bulls Cross. Continue
ahead past *The Pied Bull*. Later the pavement changes side before
reaching the entrance to Myddleton House opposite Turkey Street.

Turn left into Turkey Street. At the Great Cambridge Road
junction go through the subway on the left to continue along Turkey
Street to the station.

Historical Notes

Turkey Street: The origin of the name is a mystery. The earliest
spelling is 'Tokestrete' in the 15th century and 'Turkey Street'
appears on early 19th century maps . The village stream is known
as the 'Turkey brook'. One pub is called *The Turkey* but the older
Plough has recently become part of the Roast Inn chain. The
Turkey Street Mission serves as the only church.

Forty Hall, once known as 'Four Tree Hall', was built in the early 1630s for Sir Nicholas Rainton, a Lord Mayor of London. In the 19th century it was owned by the Meyer family and Christian Meyer built Forty Hill's Jesus church after his children had rebelled against walking to Enfield church on a hot Sunday morning. The mansion is open as a museum daily except Mondays; free. Two haycrops are cut each year in the meadows.

The New River is an artificial watercourse, cut under the direction of Sir Hugh Myddleton between 1609 and 1613, to bring water from the clean end of the river Lee near Hertford to London. The collection point was New River Head in Clerkenwell, now the Thames Water Authority headquarters. The river, which will soon become redundant as a water supply, was at first opposed by landowners, but James I gave his support despite falling into the icy water during an inspection of work.

The Crown & Tinker: The name recalls James I's journey from Scotland in 1603 to accept the English throne. Among the welcoming crowd near here was a tinker, who asked how the new King would be recognised. He was told that James would be the only man still wearing his hat and, on looking around, the tinker realised that everyone was bareheaded except for the stranger.

Theobalds Park: The original house stood to the east of the Great Cambridge Road in Theobalds Lane and was visited by Elizabeth I some 15 times. This was James I's last stopping place on his journey from Scotland and in 1607 he swapped Hatfield for Lord Salisbury's Theobalds. The King died here and Charles I was proclaimed King at the gate before setting out for London. The house was pulled down under Cromwell and the present mansion west of the New river dates from 1763. Its most famous occupant was the brewer Sir Henry Bruce Meux, who had London's Temple Bar erected at the northern entrance to his estate, where the arch still remains in a crumbling state. The house, purchased by Middlesex County Council in 1938, is now a college.

Bulls Cross was known as 'Bedell's Cross' in the 15th century, when Bullsmoor Lane met the village further north to form a crossroads with Whitewebbs Lane and the Roman road from London to York, known as Ermine Street. The lane was moved south at the request of former owners of Capel Manor, a 17th century house set in parkland which now includes the *Which?* magazine Trials Garden. The grounds are open Mondays to Fridays and summer weekends, with an admission charge. Gardening writer Frances Perry, who still lives in the village grew up in *The Pied Bull*, a former Enfield Chase kennels which became a pub in 1790.

Myddleton House, named after Sir Hugh of New river fame, was built in 1815 on the site of an earlier residence. The famous gardener EA Bowles was born here in 1865 and remained until his death in 1954, when the house was still without electricity or a telephone. The garden, now home of the National Iris Collection, retains such Bowles' features as the rock garden and an oddities corner, which includes contorted hazel known as 'Harry Lauder's Walking Stick'. Other attractions are the dry loop of the New river, Enfield's old market cross and Edward VII's pew from Sandringham church. The house is now the Lee Valley Regional Park Authority's headquarters and the garden is open on weekdays and certain summer Sunday afternoons (phone 0992 717711 for dates).